SASAKAWA

The Warrior for Peace
the Global Philanthropist

SASAKAWA

The Warrior for Peace
the Global Philanthropist

Edited by

PAULA DAVENTRY

PERGAMON PRESS

OXFORD · NEW YORK · TORONTO · SYDNEY · PARIS · FRANKFURT

U.K.	Pergamon Press Ltd., Headington Hill Hall, Oxford OX3 0BW, England
U.S.A.	Pergamon Press Inc., Maxwell House, Fairview Park, Elmsford, New York 10523, U.S.A.
CANADA	Pergamon Press Canada Ltd., Suite 104, 150 Consumers Road, Willowdale, Ontario M2J 1P9, Canada
AUSTRALIA	Pergamon Press (Aust.) Pty. Ltd., P.O. Box 544, Potts Point, N.S.W. 2011, Australia
FRANCE	Pergamon Press SARL, 24 rue des Ecoles, 75240 Paris, Cedex 05, France
FEDERAL REPUBLIC OF GERMANY	Pergamon Press GmbH, Hammerweg 6, D-6242 Kronberg-Taunus, Federal Republic of Germany

First edition 1981
Reprinted 1983

British Library Cataloguing in Publication Data
Sasakawa
1. Sasakawa, Ryoichi
2. Philanthropists — Biography
I. Daventry, Paula
361.7'6'0924   HV28.S—/
ISBN 0 08 028126 5 (Flexicover)

Printed in Great Britain by A. Wheaton & Co. Ltd., Exeter

Foreword

by the Rt. Hon. Edward Heath, MBE, MP, House of Commons

It is right that the life and work of Ryoichi Sasakawa should be made as widely known as possible across the world by this revealing biography. Although a household name in Japan he has yet to receive proper recognition amongst the people of other countries. Yet he has devoted his life's work to both national and international causes.

Ryoichi Sasakawa combines to an extraordinary degree the staunch support of a patriot for his own country with the fervour of an international enthusiast for world affairs. He is a living embodiment of the fact that there is nothing incompatible between patriotism and internationalism. Indeed he would go further than that. His philosophy demands both of himself and of his countrymen that they should play their full part in contributing to the peace and prosperity of the rest of the world.

How he has reached that intellectual conclusion and how he has been able to put it into practice as a man of action is the fascinating story of this book. A wealthy man in his early twenties, he early on had experience of military life in the Japanese Airforce and rapidly became involved in national politics as one of the founders of the Peoples Party of the Nation. He has never tried to disguise his position on the right of the political spectrum and twice, both before and after the Second World War, suffered imprisonment for it.

Both periods broadened and deepened his philosophy and after his release for the second time he set about the twin task of providing an example of hard work, enterprise and independence for his fellow countrymen, especially the young, and of making a contribution to those international organisations which he considered would best help to bring about a greater understanding between peoples of different races, backgrounds and religions.

In all this he was able to use his immense wealth to good purpose. The generosity of the most prominent American and European philanthropists is blazoned in the names of many institutions in their own countries. It is doubtful whether anyone has shown greater magnanimity to the new world organisations as well as to his national concerns than Sasakawa.

Now over eighty, Ryoichi Sasakawa presents a magnificent example of bodily and mental fitness. His energy is still immense; his personal interest in both Japanese and world affairs is intense; his determination to give young people every opportunity to make a better life for themselves enables him to overcome obstacles which have proved too daunting for lesser men; his wish to ensure a more peaceful and orderly relationship between countries shines out in all he does; his enjoyment of life, surrounded as he is by a happy family, is clear for all to see — indeed it is as infectious as his sense of humour. We can all be grateful for the efforts that Ryoichi Sasakawa has made to ease the world's ills and we may hope that many others may be led to follow his example.

Publisher's Foreword

Pergamon Press is publishing this brief illustrated book on the life and achievements of Mr. Ryoichi Sasakawa at its own risk and expense. All income from the sale of this book, including the author's royalties, will be donated to UNICEF (United Nations Children's Fund). This book is being published by Pergamon Press as a small token of appreciation for the many philanthropic efforts and enterprises that Mr. Ryoichi Sasakawa has initiated in his life-time, all of which are benefiting peace and humanity on a worldwide basis. I agree with Mr. Sasakawa when he says "The World is One Family; All Mankind are Brothers and Sisters", and I salute him as one of the world's greatest philanthropists and one of the most remarkable men whom it has been my privilege to know and with whom to work for world peace and security.

Robert Maxwell
Publisher

Acknowledgements

The Editor wishes to acknowledge the work done by Miss Nancy Hallinan, who contributed much to the preparation of the material, and her research assistant, Miss L. Sorkin, who helped so ably.

Contents

Prologue

A rope of water . . . .
Land of earthquakes and temples of stillness . . . .

Since ancient times Japanese art has given us graven images and delicate portraiture of spirits, both human and divine, in which two opposites are manifest. One spirit is calm and is appropriate to meditation; the other is fierce and is appropriate to passionate commitment. Two warring opposites: peaceful detachment and burning passion.

In writing this biography I was to discover a man who exemplifies this traditional Japanese opposition, which is so artistically rendered in temples and shrines. He is a man who is both calm and passionate. He has enduring faith in the unity of mankind, and he has a burning belief in his own personal mission—a mission to bring about world peace.

Ryoichi Sasakawa has amassed a fortune for one single purpose: global philanthropy. He feels that peace needs a foundation of universal well-being. By curing basic social ills such as malnutrition and disease, we take a step towards peace. So Sasakawa has made huge donations to the World Health Organization and other U.N. agencies as a way of fighting for peace. He is the largest single donor in the world to the United Nations.

Sasakawa is demonstrating what a single individual can do, and putting his personal beliefs into action with stunning results. His hope is that his life's work will inspire others in the world community. I am convinced that there are more Sasakawas in the world, if only they knew their potential for unstinting, unrestricted philanthropy.

1

This is why I am writing the biography of this particular man. It is my fervent hope that we will see a tidal wave of world philanthropy.

How did this son of a humble sake brewer become the multi-billionaire he is today? What drives him tirelessly toward a goal many people believe impossible? How do his many projects fit the grand design so essential for peace? What makes this man unique? This book is an attempt at answers.

Barriers of several sorts existed between Sasakawa and myself. We are people of two vastly different countries, languages, and cultures; we are people of different ages, representing a generation gap; we are people with different stations in life. He is a Japanese man of power, a multi-billionaire who belongs to a country which traditionally puts a woman in an inferior position. I am an American woman, a writer, a mother, and a resident of New York City. But despite the fact that we spoke through interpreters, which creates a certain formality, and despite the fact that our times together were all too short, we did manage to transcend the barriers between us.

The time needed for the translation of my questions and his answers provided us both with an exceptional opportunity. We sat opposite each other. We studied each other, searching our expressions, experiencing eye-contact and a growing friendship that cut through the words being carefully translated. This friendship grew despite the fact that our interviews covered some rocky territory: imprisonment, war, again imprisonment with the threat of capital punishment, the seriousness of his goal today, his self-imposed dedication to world peace.

Translating for me was Lianne Sorkin, a young American woman who studied at Waseda University in Tokyo while living with a Japanese family. Translating for Sasakawa was Maki Hamada-Woronoff, a young Japanese woman who has lived and studied in the United States. Our meetings and interviews occurred in several different places both in Japan and in America.

We first met briefly in Sasakawa's office at the Museum of Maritime Science in Tokyo. He was to officiate at a graduating class ceremony of calligraphy students through the auspices of his museum. He was also consulting with a friend about an old Japanese war plane which had recently come to the Museum from the U.S. There seemed to be no disparity between the young calligraphy students and the old dismantled airplane. This apparent diversity is a part of Sasakawa's life and is exemplified in the dichotomy of his thoroughly Japanese character.

Sasakawa was to be photographed with the students and he seemed to enjoy it. There were shouts of "smile" and "cheese". Then he posed with the teachers. There were several photographers recording the event. More shouts of "smile". Then the little ceremony was over and Sasakawa's entourage took off . . . .

Our next meeting occurred in the Japan Shipbuilding Industry Foundation offices. Here I found Sasakawa at a different job in a different environment. He was on the telephone, and I had time to wander around his office. It is from this room that so many of Sasakawa's philanthropic projects take off—on land, in the sea, and in the air. The room is a wonderful combination of museum pieces and modern office equipment. Plaques and photographs hang from the walls depicting honours which he treasures. There are desks, tables, chairs, a large couch, a coffee table on which we were served tea. Two large photographic portraits of Sasakawa stand on the floor leaning against the wall as if nobody had the time to hang them. An automatic back-massager is attached to Sasakawa's chair. Here is a man who can both relax and work at the same time. The phones ring almost ceaselessly. Male secretaries come and go. Young women bring him messages and us more tea. Sasakawa is busy. My colleague, Lianne Sorkin, and I are kept waiting. Yet suddenly our host tosses us each a huge orange. (Apparently this is one of his favourite fruits.) We are getting to know each other . . . .

Our prolonged interviews occurred in Hiratsuka, a small town near the foot of Mount Fuji. Hiratsuka is a ninety-minute drive from Tokyo, along narrow roads which twist endlessly through the hilly countryside. There were several of us in our party, and a suite of rooms had been rented for us at the Lakewood Country Club. The rooms led out onto a wide balcony which overlooked a golf course. It was spring and the grass was a particularly radiant shade of green. This inn provided us with privacy and quiet, and it was here that our most memorable conversations took place. Here we were undisturbed by secretaries, messengers, assistants and officials from various organizations. We met in a room overlooking the golf course, and sat at a long conference table.

Our last meeting was on the other side of the Pacific. It took place in San Francisco. Here was yet another opportunity to see Sasakawa. We watched the usual fanfare at the airport upon his arrival, and later that same day we saw him address a large audience of Japanese-Americans at the Japan Cultural Centre Theatre. This was the occasion of a spectacular performance of Japanese poetry recitation and dance, in which Sasakawa's wife, Shizue, chanted and played the *biwa*, the traditional Japanese lute.

Our interviews in San Francisco took place in a hotel room suite. Here Sasakawa was in an especially buoyant mood. His recent travels had included Scandinavia, Southeast Asia, the South Pacific and the United States. He had just arrived from Los Angeles where he had received the Key to the City.

I was a true innocent when I undertook this biography. I had never been to Japan, and now I was to meet and write about one of its most powerful citizens, or, as he prefers to call himself, a world citizen who happens to be Japanese. It was my toughest assignment at interviewing, and the first time I had worked through interpreters. It was hard work, but full of surprises and excitement, lessons in manners and culture. It was an adventure. It was also an oddly spiritual journey for me.

Chapter 1

Ryoichi Sasakawa—an Overview

Ryoichi Sasakawa is a world philanthropist. He is a multi-millionaire and the millions he has created go to all kinds of worthwhile and humanitarian causes at home and abroad. He is also a strong believer in world peace and feels that his humanitarian donations in all parts of the world will help bring that about. He is a very visible figure in Japan and also a very controversial one. Outside Japan he is not widely known, although the results of some of his philanthropy have had a great effect on many people's lives. The best-known example of this is the eradication of smallpox throughout the world—Sasakawa contributed enormous sums to this particular World Health Organization programme.

The causes to which Sasakawa has contributed are myriad. He gives large and small donations to large and small organizations. For example, in 1980 he gave 4,000,000 dollars to the World Health Organization, but he also gave just over 1000 dollars to a hospital in Singapore; he gave 500,000 dollars to the Japanese Association of Argentina, but also 1800 dollars to the Japanese School of San Diego; he gave 500,000 dollars to the U.N. secretariat and 24,000 dollars to a museum in Norway. In total he gave over 7,000,000 dollars to overseas causes in 1980.

This is in fact a very small sum compared with what he donates within Japan itself. In 1979 he gave nearly 200,000,000 dollars in loans and subsidies to the shipbuilding industry, especially for the development of shipbuilding technology. He also gave 45,000,000 dollars to social welfare projects and 5,000,000 for the promotion of physical training.

All this money is handed out under the auspices of the Japan Shipbuilding Industry Foundation, a body which Sasakawa founded in 1962. It has given away, over the years, more than 12 billion dollars—more than the Ford Foundation has given. The name of the Foundation comes from Sasakawa's original interest in the rebuilding of the Japanese shipbuilding industry after its total destruction in World War II, and how his interest extended from this to international philanthropy is the story of this biography. If the Japan Shipbuilding Industry Foundation has moved from simply supporting Japanese shipbuilding into support for marine safety measures and to social welfare projects in Japan, and then on to international concerns, it is because of the influence of one man—Ryoichi Sasakawa.

Why does Ryoichi Sasakawa give away so much money to international causes? His actions are based on his strong personal belief that the world is one family and that all mankind are brothers and sisters. While many other people would adhere to this same belief, few have taken the concrete action that Sasakawa has taken to put it into effect. So for him it is not a mere platitude but the basis for his life's work.

Sasakawa sees in world philanthropy a path to universal peace. He does not see it as the only way to world peace—as he says: "There are many paths up Mount Fuji"—but he sees his own path as the creation of enormous wealth and then its distribution to the poor and needy of the earth. If other millionaires would follow suit, the sufferings of the world would be greatly alleviated, and this would help us along the path to world peace.

In a way, Sasakawa's views seem very simplistic. Many might query whether money can buy world peace. But looked at from another point of view, his views have a refreshing simplicity to them. It seems extraordinary in our unpeaceful and unstable times to find someone who dares to believe that world peace is possible, let alone that he personally can do something about it. Maybe he can have this faith because, as he says, "Somehow it seems to me that some people return to their original innocence at the end of their lives."

Sasakawa, then, dares to believe that change for the better can occur, and he himself has put his faith in the U.N., though he is very critical of the way that country delegations represent the interests of their countries as they see them rather than the interests of the international community as a whole. He speaks out too against the arms race. He says: "I think all major powers should . . . stop lending support to countries engaged in a dispute, and stop the supply and sale of armaments . . . . (They) should carry out a 10% reduction of their military budgets and put this money to the solution of the population problem . . . ."

Within Japan his greatest interest at the moment is the promotion of his Blue Sea and Green Land (B & G) Foundation. He sees this organization as a way of countering today's materialism. "We are losing the meaning of the spiritual and the natural life . . . . Even though we Japanese are now prospering to the point where we are a major economic power in the world, we may be destroying ourselves in other ways." The B & G Foundation was set up in 1973 with the aim of promoting the healthy development of the minds and bodies of young people.

Sasakawa is clearly doing a great deal of good both inside and outside Japan, and the views he expresses must be acceptable to many who hear of them. Why then is he unpopular with so many Japanese, and why is the Japanese press so frequently critical of him? There are two main reasons. Firstly, people dislike the way the Japan Shipbuilding Industry Foundation (JSIF) acquires its money. Secondly, people dislike the power that Sasakawa can wield in Japan.

The money that pours into the coffers of JSIF comes directly as a small percentage of profits from gambling on motor boat racing. This is the most popular form of gambling in Japan today. Sasakawa himself does not gamble, and reportedly does not like gambling, yet presumably he feels that in the case of motor boat racing it is justified because of the uses to which the profits are put. Others do not agree. When Sasakawa was awarded a distinguished honour by the Emperor—the First Order of Merit, the Order of the Sacred Treasure—for his long meritorious services, some previous holders of decorations returned theirs because they disliked the fact that those meritorious services were made possible by gambling. Then again Sasakawa spends 17,000,000 dollars annually on TV advertising, and while many of the commercials extol the virtues of the healthful way of life, good deeds, filial piety, the B & G Foundation, and respect for the Japanese flag, their real message is the promotion of gambling. Japanese critics feel that the message "Profits from motorboat races go to charity" is somewhat hypocritical. (They are not mollified by the fact that Sasakawa himself appears in many of the ads where he is seen running over green fields with children to promote the B & G Foundation. Critics feel that Sasakawa is using the ads for self-promotion.)

Not only does Sasakawa's organization, JSIF, make its money from gambling, he himself has acquired a great deal of power through his control of the motorboat racing industry. It is difficult for those from outside Japan to appreciate just what this power means. But he does have a monopoly on the most popular gambling sport in Japan. No one else has a remotely similar position. There is more than one person controlling gambling on horse racing, bicycle racing and car racing, the other popular sports on which gambling takes place in Japan. The amount of wealth created, some 2,000 billion yen or 10 billion US dollars at present rate (accumulated between 1952 and 1980), puts Sasakawa in a quite extraordinary position.

There are other manifestations of Sasakawa's power that are peculiarly Japanese. In Japan he is known as a *kuromaku*. *Kuromaku* are behind-the-scenes manipulators of political power. They can make or break prime ministers without themselves being in politics. Richard Halloran, writing in the *New York Times* (2 July, 1974) said: "They continue to exert enormous influence but it is slowly slipping away as their time passes and a new generation looks to others . . . . *Kuromaku* need front men and many of their front men have died or retired from power." Sasakawa was "the last of a breed".

Sasakawa is reputed to have helped both Eisaku Sato and Kakuei Tanaka to become prime minister. He himself has said:

"*Kuromaku* are only useful in a society where laws are ambiguous and law-enforcement agencies weak . . . from now on laws and institutions will be strong enough to make Japanese society function smoothly without intermediaries." (Interview with Kenneth Labich, reported in *Newsweek*, 10 January, 1977.)

But there is no doubt that he has exercised power in this way.

Given his wealth and influence, Sasakawa is important enough to be made chairman of many different organizations. Through his own interest in karate (he is a ninth-dan himself), he has become Chairman of the World Union of Karate-do Federations. Japanese people tend to identify strongly with their leaders and Sasakawa himself claims to enjoy the loyalty of one million Japanese through this one organization. He is also a patron of judo and kendo societies, and a plethitude of other organizations from the Japanese Disabled Veterans Association to the Japan Civil Aviation Promotion Foundation through the Japan Musical Culture Foundation. Through the chairmanship of these organizations he enjoys a great deal of support and he is accused of having at his disposal a "private army".

Sasakawa, despite the directness and simplicity of his views on world peace, is not a simple man. Sometimes it seems he would like to appear so. "When I was a child", he says, "I used to like the company of adults; now as an old man I prefer the company of children." But this man who likes children most of all and who thinks all men are brothers the world over, also effectively controls a vast financial empire and successfully operates in the subtle world of Japanese politics. This biography does not attempt to show that one side or the other is correct. Both sides are true. In this biography we try to look at just what kind of person Sasakawa is, and then we look at his life history in detail and show just how this complex person and his views have evolved.

Chapter 2

The Man

Ryoichi Sasakawa is a small but quite heavily built man. He has a firm taut body and a bouncy step. His whole demeanour is one of purposefulness. There are no wasted motions. He is an octagenarian who looks as if he were a vigorous man in his early sixties.

Many Westerners have been told about the "inscrutable" Japanese facial expression. Sasakawa's face is a lively contradiction to this cliché. His large eyes are light brown. They are capable of a mischievous twinkle, then a sudden change as if he were exploring a new idea and wondering how to express it. Remarkably, for an 81-year-old, he has no need for glasses.

In a Western suit, he could be mistaken for any Japanese business executive. But for everyday working he usually wears the zip-up running jacket of his Blue Sea and Green Land Foundation. This jacket is white with four coloured stripes round the midriff and a red rising sun—symbol of Japan—on the back. Sasakawa's personal creed is inscribed around the sun: *The world is one family: all mankind are brothers and sisters.* For ceremonial functions, Sasakawa puts on traditional Japanese costume.

When talking informally, Sasakawa's short-fingered and expressive hands are constantly in motion. He gestures with his index finger, frequently touching his nose. (This is a polite Japanese way of saying "I".) Often he spreads the fingers of his hands, palm open and outwards and then may make an arc-like motion with both hands as if embracing the world.

When seated he sits with legs apart, feet firmly on the ground, sometimes elbows on his knees and his hands clasped in front of him.

At all times his posture is upright, whether seated or standing. He is usually full of good spirits.

How has this genial person acquired control of a vast financial empire and how does he continue to control it at the age of 81 along with all his other commitments? Firstly, he clearly has, even by Japanese standards, an exceptional capacity to work. An ordinary work day begins something like this:

"During the summer I am up at five in the morning. If the weather is good, I jog four kilometers every day. Jogging is an activity I encourage. It's part of our B & G sports programme. Jogging activates the circulation system, and allows man a happy relationship with nature. In the winter I usually get up later and jog around six o'clock. After jogging I eat breakfast about seven. This generally consists of yogurt, Japanese soup and some fruit. I don't like eggs. But at every meal I take my share of natural vitamins. At seven-thirty I leave for the office. By nine o'clock I've already had four appointments. I 'punch in' at various places throughout the day."

For someone who has such a large personal fortune and absolutely no need to work, his driving energy is astonishing. Even some of his young entourage feel the strain of his schedule. In a thirty-day period in 1980 he crisscrossed both the Pacific and the Atlantic, travelling from Tokyo to Los Angeles (to receive the key), to San Francisco (to host poetry recitations), then back home to Japan for a week's business agenda. Next to Stockholm (to be present at the meeting of the International Federation for the Institutes of Advanced Studies, under the auspices of the King of Sweden). Then to meet explorer and archaeologist Dr. Thor Heyerdahl to discuss mutual oceanic interest. Next to Oslo, where he went to express his thanks to officials of the Almondsen Collection for the loan of some two thousand artifacts from the South Pole expedition. Then back to Tokyo, where he continued his usual pace without missing a beat. It seems to be no exaggeration to describe him as a man in his prime.

One of the reasons that Sasakawa can keep up such an astonishing pace must be his personal contentment with life. He told me: "Oh yes, I am a happy man. I have no time that is wasted. Like a little child, there is never a blank time that is wasted."

"Have you ever had self-doubts or felt helpless?" I asked.

"No, never. Nothing is impossible if you devote your whole soul to it. Then anything is possible."

He clearly has a great deal of optimism in his make-up, and also a lot of self-assurance.

He obviously thrives on challenge and opposition. He has twice in his life been imprisoned. (We look at the reasons why when we consider his life history. Suffice it to say here that on neither occasion was he found guilty of anything.) On both occasions, Sasakawa seems to have turned the experience of imprisonment into a positive and useful event in his life. Both times, he seems to have seen fate at work, and to have accepted his situation with equanimity if not cheerfulness (which, as he said, annoyed the prison warders). During his second term in prison, he began to think about his own personal need to work towards world peace. So prison was a time for thought and for regeneration.

When I asked one employee of Sasakawa's what his most impressive quality was, the man replied immediately "his vision". Sasakawa's success in the everyday world must in part be attributed to his ability to look beyond the everyday and to aim at a goal which has been created in his own imagination. He seems to have the ability to pursue this kind of goal against all the odds and with a driving energy. When he emerged from prison at the end of the Second World War at the age of 49, under the stigma of having been a war criminal, it would have taken a very farsighted observer to visualize him as the world philanthropist we know today. But Sasakawa had vision and had faith in himself and so was able to start along his path towards world peace.

Another quality of Sasakawa's that must have contributed towards his success is his ability to go on learning. He believes firmly that as one gets older, one should make friends with younger people. He personally has done just this. Many of his employees at the Japan Shipbuilding Industry Foundation are young. He is also very concerned that the young should have a healthy and positive future—which explains his current preoccupation with the Blue Sea and Green Land Foundation.

Apparently by Japanese standards, Sasakawa is very democratic. One young employee told me that when they are being driven in the big black Mercedes-Benz—riding from appointment to appointment—both employer and employee sit in the back seat. "He wants me to feel like an associate, or a partner, and not a subordinate. And it's much easier to talk when we're sitting right next to each other. There's absolutely no generation gap." Sasakawa also told me: "I usually eat lunch with my people at the JSIF offices. We have a canteen on the top floor of our building. (We have no such thing as an executive dining room)." However, this democrat does have an autocratic streak. When asked what Sasakawa's negative characteristics were, one employee replied with a smile: "That man can really yell when he gets mad."

Sasakawa exercises a great deal of personal magnetism, especially for his young employees. I saw this very clearly when he addressed an audience in San Francisco. They were Japanese who had come to hear a recitation of songs of Japanese spirit and nature and Sasakawa gave the introductory address. I really enjoyed the way he projected his voice and cracked jokes, at the same time maintaining a dignified posture before the microphone. The audience was very attentive to him.

At this same concert I had another unexpected view of him—of an almost childlike enthusiasm. At the end of the concert he was so thrilled with the applause that he crawled out from under the curtain once it had come down for the final time and waved his arms about in a lasso-throwing motion as if to say to the audience *"Banzai!!!"* (Victory!!!) We all responded. This childlike enthusiasm and generous nature underlies his philanthropy just as much as his serious concern for world peace.

So far we have looked at Sasakawa only as a successful businessman and philanthropist. What about his personal life outside of work? Sasakawa told me:

"I think of myself as an ordinary working man who puts in a long day. But I admit to one exception. I work three hundred and sixty-five days of the year. I take no holidays." And he has told another interviewer: "When I die, that's when I will take my vacation" *(New Nation*, 17 March, 1980).

"Don't you ever relax?" I asked.

"Relax? When I go home, theoretically I can relax. But still there are so many letters to answer. I relax when I sleep.

"When I get insomnia and can't sleep, then I get up. It may be two or three in the morning. I get up and go to my desk and begin writing. I work on my newspaper column."

When I asked him about our Western forms of relaxation—movies, theatre, concerts, museums, reading, not to mention spectator sports—he swiftly shook his head and his right hand gestured a negative.

"I'm a man who works all the time. I don't read books or magazines, and I only look at the headlines of newspapers. I know almost everybody in political and business circles here in Japan. We speak over the phone . . . ."

Later when we met in San Francisco I accidentally discovered an innocuous relaxation of his. On the couch were playing cards—a game of solitaire. Since he was not there ready to meet us, we respected his game and did not move the cards. When he came in, he smiled and gathered the cards together.

I asked him once about reincarnation, and he said that one reason he gave himself no holidays was that he must have been very lazy in a previous life. When I reminded him of this comment he laughed.

"I only said that as a joke. All I know is that I must work, and I really don't know why. I only know that I am fulfilled and happy in my work. What more can a man ask?"

Sasakawa did once boast to a reporter that he had conquered more than 500 women, so he must have devoted some time and energy to this end. Perhaps he now regrets this remark, and certainly his attitude to sex seems to have changed. He told me:

"Not too long ago I was speaking with one of the elderly monks at a temple which I had helped over some rough times. While I was waiting for the High Priest, this monk and I had a long conversation which covered many subjects. One of them was sex. We two octagenarians had lived very different lives.

"This man had been celibate all his life. On the other hand I had enjoyed many women. And I had never for a moment thought I might regret these experiences. Now during this intimate conversation with this monk I looked back on my past, and what it meant to me. I rather surprised myself when I found myself envying this celibate man. I told my friend, 'You are a lucky man.' This was the first time I had realized the enormous physical and emotional drain of energy from love affairs. At the age of twenty, one does not think of such matters! Now I envied this monk his celibacy. I told him, 'I fell in love many, many times. One pays a price. I used up a lot of time and sexual energy. Now that I think about it, I'd like that time and energy back!' "

What about Sasakawa's underlying philosophy? I asked him about his religious beliefs.

"Do you believe in the power of prayer?"

"Yes, I most certainly do and I thank God for his merciful answers."

"Do you feel that you have divine guidance for your mission of peace here on this earth?"

"Yes. I don't know whose voice it is, but there are times when I hear a very clear message."

"Do you believe in the hereafter?"

"Yes, I believe in the after world. The soul never dies."

Sasakawa was brought up in a very religious household. Of Buddhism he now says, "I agree with my friend Yoshiyasu Nagayama (Chief Priest of the Kasuga Shrine in Nara) who describes Buddhism as a religion that stresses philanthropy and intelligence. I believe that Buddhism is related to Christianity in many ways—particularly in the theory of universal love. When I speak of God, I mean a universal God. His spirit is all about us—everywhere. It is in the air we breathe, it is in the earth, and in the seas. I feel a strong sense of awe about God's magnificence in the force of water . . . ."

Sasakawa's beliefs now seem to centre on water. He says that he no longer reads the teachings of Buddha. "I respect the religion, and for what it can do for the people. But I don't like the formalities." What he calls his "waterology" is now the guiding force in his life.

Water has always been important to him. This goes back to his father's influence on him in childhood. He said:

"I learned a great deal from my father. He attached importance to water. He used to tell me, 'When you have water or light, stop for a moment and think about how you would feel if you didn't have either water or light. It is when you are in the present that you can be grateful for what you have.' " His father's words have stayed with him all his life. Sasakawa is very much a person who lives " in the now" and appreciates the blessings of the present.

Not only has water taught him about the importance of the present, it is quite literally the basis of the fortune made by the Japan Ship-building Industry Foundation—motor boat racing takes place on water. Sasakawa has a printed pamphlet which explains his beliefs and on his visiting card is printed the following:

- Water gives the animate their vital sources of life.
- Water flows tirelessly seeking its way forward.
- Water intrepidly overcomes anything in its way, yet it conforms to the shape of the vessel which contains it.
- Water is pure in itself, cleansing anything impure, yet capable of embracing both pure and impure.
- Water turns into power and light, thereby serving production and livelihood boundlessly in expectation of no reward.
- Water fills an ocean and evaporates into clouds, then becomes rain, snow or hail without losing any of its basic traits.
- To follow the spirit of water is to foster peace.

Chapter 3

Gonta (Brat)

He is as good
as he is wicked.
(Japanese proverb)

Ryoichi Sasakawa was born on 4 May 1899 in Ononhara, Toyokawa Village, Mishima County in Osaka Prefecture. Onohara was then a rural area of low rolling hills and rice paddies. The countryside was fairly flat with an occasional forest darkening the horizon. Mount Minoo rose above it to an altitude of 500 metres. The village below was a peaceful place.

I visited the old Sasakawa home, and though Toyokawa Village is now part of Minoo City, the house itself and the immediate neighbourhood remain very much as they were eighty years ago. The houses in the street are similar but not identical and together they form a homogenous neighbourhood.

The courtyard and front entrance of the Sasakawa house are shaded by a large pine tree which is a blessing in the intense summer heat. The courtyard itself is plain earth with a small path made of square stone slabs. The whole provides an atmosphere of calm and serenity.

The house is still occupied by the Sasakawa family—Ryoichi's sister and her daughter, son-in-law and new granddaughter. Ryoichi's sister told me that the room in which we were entertained had not changed in any way since Ryoichi was a small boy. There were traditional *tatami* mats (straw-covered reed mats) on the floor, *shoji* screens (paper covered lattice screens) for walls, above them a 12 inch beam supporting a further 2 foot of wall, which has a subtle glis-

17

ten in its sandy-gold colour and which appears not to be supporting anything, but floating in space with no purpose other than its own beauty.

Ryoichi Sasakawa was the second child and first son of Tsurukichi Sasakawa and Teru Sasakawa. They had in all seven children, four daughters and three sons. Sadly, three of the baby girls died shortly after birth. The four who lived to be adult were Ryoichi, Shunji (son), Yoshiko (daughter) and Ryohei (son). Even these children were not all healthy. Shunji was always sickly and had asthma.

Ryoichi's father, Tsurukichi, ran a sake brewery and his mother actively assisted in the business. The Sasakawas owned their own home and had three domestic servants, as well as employing migrant sake workers when necessary for the business. The servants did all the household chores, looked after each new baby and cooked meals for the migrant workers.

Ryoichi told me: "My father believed in the frugal life, and my parents seemed content. We had all the necessities of life. We had a roof over our heads, three nourishing meals a day, and daily bathing."

Although merchants at this time were important in village life, they were not considered to be aristocrats. However, the Sasakawas are descended from a distinguished lineage. This is shown from an old photograph they have which shows an ancestor wearing a sword. Before the Meiji restoration in 1868, any family that was allowed to use a surname and wear sidearms was of distinguished descent. Interestingly this is still of a certain importance in the meritocratic Japan of today.

The Sasakawas were religious people. Although business was conducted in their house all the time, it took place within a strong spiritual atmosphere. They had a fine *Butsudan* (Buddhist house altar) which is still in the Sasakawa house today. It is 6 foot high with gold painted folding doors behind which are placed holy objects. Small daily offerings are still left there for the departed spirits. (The day I was there the offerings were an orange and a slice of pastry.) Statues of Buddha, incense holders, tiny lamps are part of the altar, and there are black-lacquered drawers at the base. The whole room in which the altar stands is a work of art which, in its traditional simplicity and beauty, creates a spiritual ambience. It was in this atmosphere of beauty and spirituality, as well as commercial enterprise, that Ryoichi Sasakawa spent his childhood.

From my interviews with Ryoichi's brother and sister, Ryohei and Yoshiko, I gathered that theirs was a happy family. The parents were very strict but kindly. Sasakawa remembers them less fondly. When I asked him about them, he jumped up from his chair and immediately began to demonstrate a particularly traumatic occasion. He is a vivid and dramatic raconteur. He spread his hands with his fingers outstretched over an imaginary fire. . . .

"My father was a very strict man, and my mother was strict too. We called her a 'she-demon'. . . . When I was three or four years old, I would put my hands over the open *hibachi* (charcoal brazier) to warm them. Every time I got my hands over the heat, my father would slap them. I didn't know why he did this. I felt hurt and unjustly punished. Then my mother explained to me that if I put my hands over the whole *hibachi*, I would take up all the heat; there wouldn't be any heat for the others in the room. In this way I learned the importance of sharing."

Perhaps the different way the different children remember their parents is accounted for by their different temperaments. Yoshiko speaks very fondly of Ryoichi and says he was always kind to her. Occasionally, she remembers, he would cook the family's meals when their mother was busy selling sake, and the houseboy and two women servants were busy with the migrant sake workers. However, the dominant impression that Ryoichi himself and others give is of a *gonta*, the local dialect word for a mischievous brat. A typical exploit is described by Ryoichi:

"When I was a small child I would go secretly and look into all the little drawers of our *Butsudan*. Of course, this was forbidden. On one occasion I found a piece of glass in a wooden box in one of the little drawers. It was like a glass sheet, about two inches square. When I held it up to the light, it looked like a picture of a monster. I was caught then and there. After my punishment, I was told that it was the negative of the photo of my grandfather."

Another incident that Ryoichi related in great detail shows that although he was a *gonta* and although he felt his parents were over-strict, nevertheless he respected his parents and learnt from them.

When I asked him towards the end of our interviews what were the turning points in his life, this particular incident was one of the three major turning points that he chose.

One day, he told me, when he was 12 years old, he decided to skip school with several of his classmates. (He hated music class.) They headed for the shrine hidden in the forest on a hill outside the village. Here they spent the morning climbing the shrine and the surrounding trees, chasing rabbits and playing war games. Suddenly it began to rain. The boys hid inside the shrine building until the rain let up. They ate their lunches and went home at the usual time, joining their schoolmates who were also on their way home.

On his return home, Ryoichi felt a strange silence in the house. Suddenly his father grabbed him by the collar, and without a word pushed him into the brewery warehouse and locked the door. Ryoichi felt baffled by his father's actions, but he was a young extrovert, and characteristically made the best of his predicament. He opened the skylight on the second floor and discovered an earthenware bowl of sweets. This was his mother's hidden store and he helped himself generously. Then he fell asleep. Eventually his mother crept into the warehouse. She did her best to get her son to apologize, but since he had no idea why he was being treated like this, he turned his back on her, and again went to sleep.

At night-fall Tsurukichi shook him awake and dragged him outside into the yard. Here he bound his son's hands behind his back and tied his feet together with rope. The boy screamed at his father in outrage. And the father shouted back, insisting on an apology. By now it was past ten o'clock. Father and son glared at each other. Then the old man untied the boy and ordered him to go to the cemetery and come back with an incense stick from the crematorium. This meant walking through dark woods toward the resting place of the dead. Ryoichi obeyed briskly and returned, offering in hand. Again his father insisted on an apology. Again Ryoichi refused. Tsurukichi, in utter exasperation, ordered his son to go to the Kasuga shrine and bring back one of the sacred paper strips hanging there. The shrine is in a forest not far from the cemetery. As he stepped through the *Torii* gate he felt strange chills, and his heart began to hammer against his ribs. He groped for the sacred paper, found it, and ran all the way home.

Here he discovered his mother in tears, and his father's dark eyes full of anger. Now, at last, he was told why he was being punished. When it had started to rain, his mother had sent one of the servants to the school with an umbrella; and the servant had returned with the information that Ryoichi had not gone to school at all that day.

Suddenly the father put his hand on the boy's shoulder.

"Ryoichi, when you lie or do anything bad, even if no one is watching you, you will be found out sooner or later. It doesn't matter how secretly you behave. People who lie are unworthy of the human race. Remember that in the house of Sasakawa there are no liars."

Now his mother spoke. "Remember also that whenever you do something wrong, God knows and you know. Now go and pray at our altar."

These admonitions from his parents have stayed with him to this day.

Whatever Ryoichi's parents may have felt about his rebellious behaviour, his peers liked it. When he started school at the age of seven he was already an acknowledged leader. The children's favourite game was war. They made guns from young bamboo shoots, and Ryoichi was always the general, with older boys under his command. According to Yasuiri Sasakawa, his old friend and distant cousin, these war games were an important part of their growing up. He told me that Ryoichi was indeed always the general, but he was also protective of the younger boys.

In fact, despite the fact that Ryoichi was a *gonta*, there were many positive sides to his character that were already being demonstrated. He was, for example, unusually imaginative. For example, he pulled a rope through a rice bag, transforming it into a makeshift "tank". Then he made the other children pull it. He was equally ingenious at hoop rolling. Scorning the thin small hoops that his companions used, he surprised everyone by rolling a giant hoop which he had removed from a rice vat.

Another positive aspect of his character, and one which has shown itself throughout his life, was already evident when he was a child. All the children were strictly brought up and were severely punished if they misbehaved. According to his old friend, Yasuiri Sasakawa, Ryoichi was never afraid of punishment. At an early age he seems to have had the character to accept punishment, no matter how harsh, a quality that was of great use to him in later years as we shall see.

Of himself as a child, Ryoichi now says: "No matter what I did, I did it well! One of the reasons I did so well was because I was never anxious to win. I just wanted to enjoy myself . . ." This quality seems to be true of him even today.

Ryoichi finished his formal education at primary school at thirteen as was usual in those days. When Ryoichi graduated, the school principal warned his father about the dangers of further study. The principal's theory was that too much education might create problems.

"He told my father, 'You don't know what sort of a monster you might create.' By "monster" he meant a radical. I was enough of a rascal in those days to warrant all sorts of dire predictions."

In fact, his father decided to send him to Shonenji Temple in Minoo. Here he received a strict education from Priest Harada and perfected his Chinese calligraphy studies.

"I was there on and off from the age of thirteen to seventeen. At the temple I learned Chinese calligraphy, and I wrote poetry."

These calligraphy lessons may account for his interest in the calligraphy classes he sponsors today.

What of the future? Despite all his enjoyment of play and all his mischievous behaviour, Ryoichi had always worked alongside his parents. As the first son he was being trained in the family business, a common tradition. His parents and Ryoichi himself had no higher expectations for him at that time. That this bright but unruly lad would one day be the guest of the King of Sweden would have been considered an outlandish fantasy, had such a fantasy ever entered their minds. He was the son of a successful sake brewer, and as such he would inherit the business.

Tsurukichi Sasakawa was a man of considerable business acumen, a fact that the young Ryoichi was to appreciate fully only once he came into his inheritance. Interestingly, he was taught by his father not to be too profit-minded. "He told me he could make more money by selling in bulk than by selling in small quantities on the retail level. Yet we *did* sell in small quantities in our front hall. And I knew that my father sold our sake to our friends and neighbours at a generous discount. He told me that the most important thing in life is to offer friendship to others."

Ryoichi enjoyed selling sake in the entrance hall. In those days, sake buyers brought their own wooden containers which were then filled with sake according to their requests. Ryoichi, using the wooden measuring box, always gave them a little extra. The Sasakawa employees, of course, could not do this. So a great many customers bought their sake when word got around that Ryoichi was serving. He was doing as his father said, and offering friendship to others.

Tsurukichi Sasakawa was not only a businessman, he was also a farmer, a village leader and a progressive thinker and he possessed many good qualities that his son would later emulate. Ryoichi told me of one way in which his father helped the village.

Nearly every summer the village of Toyokawa suffered a crippling drought which affected not only the rice paddies but all fields of agriculture. It was so bad that the villagers described their barren land as being "Dried up by the light from the moon". Tsurukichi Sasakawa grappled with this problem and finally, with inspiration and stubborn persuasion, managed to arrange irrigation from the neighbouring town of Minoo. Thereafter, water flowed through a series of irrigation conduits from Minoo into Toyokawa. This irrigation made possible wet-field rice cultivation, and double-cropping, a common practice of Japanese farmers since ancient times. It also saved the village from the effects of regular drought.

When the irrigation conduits were completed, and precious water flowed into their land, the villagers were so grateful that they wished to erect a monument to Tsurukichi. Sasakawa remembers this occasion very well. "My father, instead of accepting this honour, told the villagers that he would be most pleased if they used the money for a more useful purpose. He suggested raising a wall around the pond which served as a reservoir. He said, 'A monument could be destroyed. Instead, each of you may build a monument in your heart which nothing can destroy.' "

It was under the influence of this harsh but wise father that Ryoichi grew up. He listened and learned from his father and from his mother. In his tranquil home his spiritual nature was fostered.

Chapter 4

Pilot / Politician / Millionaire

I have bought bread
I have been given
  Red roses:
How happy I am
To hold
  Both in my hands

(Kitahara Hakushu, from *Springs of Oriental Wisdom*)

One day a single plane flew over the blue tiled roofs of Toyokawa village. Ryoichi saw it. Two days later he learned that the pilot had crashed and died. He felt a strange mixture of emotions; he was both shocked at the tragedy, and inspired by it. He also felt that familiar emotion, challenge, but this time with some new intensity. He was determined to become a pilot himself, one who would never crash. He quickly saw the future of aviation.

"The only pilot in Japan at that time who did stunt flying and barnstorming was a man called Kiyoshi Nishide. He had studied flying in the United States, and brought his own biplane back to Japan. His photo was in all the newspapers. I also read that this famous plane was being held by the Japanese Customs—at a bonded warehouse in Yokohama—because Nishide did not have the necessary money to pay the duty tax . . . .

"I was seventeen years old. I knew I needed to meet this pilot, and I persuaded my father to put up the money needed to release the plane. At first he objected strenuously. Who was I to spend family income on some flyer? We argued for a long time. I think I succeeded in persuading him to put up the money because he was receptive to new ideas. He was an old man, but he was still a progressive person.

24

Awarded the First Class Order of the Sacred Treasure

Ryoichi Sasakawa receives Scroll of Appreciation from UN
Secretary-General Waldheim at UN headquarters, April 19, 1979

Scroll of Appreciation presented to Sasakawa
from UN Secretary-General Waldheim

Sasakawa and Astronaut Neil Armstrong

With Mrs. MacArthur, widow of General Douglas MacArthur

Bust of Sasakawa at WHO headquarters

International War Memorial built by Ryoichi Sasakawa
as a symbol of his quest for lasting world peace

Speedboat racing

Ryoichi Sasakawa on a racing motorboat at the Motosu Motorboat
Racers' Training Institute

Sasakawa jogging early in the morning with children

"Emily" returned to Japan

Surrounded by children in front of the Saturn 1B
Rocket at the Space Science Exposition, 1978

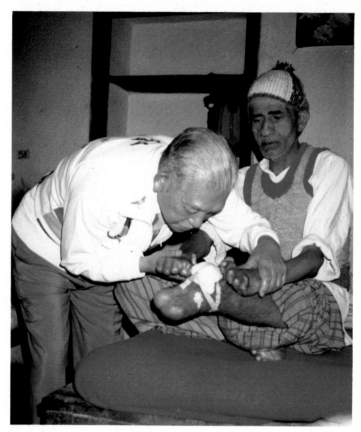

Sasakawa with a leper

Overall view of Okinawa Marine Recreation Center
of the B & G Foundation

Overall view of Museum of Maritime Science

Smashing ten stacked roof tiles December 4, 1977;
at the Nihon Budo-kan

Sasakawa in formal attire

A family shrine

We agreed that airplanes soared into the future.

"Some months later Nishide came to our house, travelling by rickshaw. When he saw us he had tears in his eyes, he was so grateful. Soon he and I were great friends. This was enormously flattering to me, because Nishide was thirty-two or thirty-three years old, at least fourteen years older than me. . . .

"When Nishide left our home, I wanted to follow him. I knew my father would not approve, so I decided to run away. But before I left home I confided in my mother. Finally she accepted my decision, and even went so far as to give me a hundred yen to make the journey. This was an act of courage I deeply appreciated. Both of us knew that after I'd gone it would be my mother's role to deal with my father's anger and calm him down. . . .

"My second confidant was my friend Uoshima. He agreed to carry my few necessary belongings in a big *furoshiki* (scarf for carrying things) to the station platform. This is how I managed to escape the house without my father or any of the family or servants knowing it."

Today this old friend still remembers the occasion. He is also 81 years old, and lives down the street from the Sasakawa family home. His grin is as mischievous today as it must have been on that day when he helped Ryoichi run away from home.

We spoke briefly together, and he laughed out loud, remembering those days.

Ryoichi's mother, although she'd helped her son leave home, did not know his whereabouts. Eventually, his father found out through Uoshima where his son had gone. It was to Wakayama Prefecture where Nishide was living.

Here, Ryoichi worked for Nishide, repairing and maintaining the fragile early planes. And learning to fly.

His ability to fly proved very useful when, in 1918 at the age of 19, two years after he had run away from home, he was drafted for military service. He was assigned to the Army Air Corps and was sent to their base at Kagamihara. Here he underwent the vigorous training of a pilot, at the same time enjoying the rare status of being a member of the élite Air Corps. He entered as a second class private, was soon promoted to first class private, and during his second year of duty became a first class private with sergeant's responsibilities. Apparently these two years were happy ones. He did not once go home to visit his family.

"The Air Corps was my family", he said. "And my airplane was my sweetheart."

Perhaps one of the reasons he enjoyed these years was the preferential treatment he received. An old friend of his father who used to visit the Sasakawa home to play *go,* was the leader of the First Air Corps at Tokorozawa near the Sasakawa home. A word from this man to the leader of his unit was sufficient to have him well looked after.

In almost every unit, however, there is a tyrant. And there is no escaping him. A warrant officer called Oda had worked his way up from the bottom to become a first-rate bully. In those days an airplane engine had to be started manually by turning the propeller. This can be dangerous, and most of the cadets were afraid of getting wounded by the downward sweep of one of the blades. Apparently Oda made the most of their fears, jeering at the men, calling them cowards, threatening them with dishonourable discharge (loss of face), and reminding them just what a propeller blade can do if you don't get out of its way.

"I was confident about my abilities. After all, I'd been trained by Nishide. And so I knew the importance of identifying with the plane. Treat your plane like a sweetheart, and she'll behave like one."

Oda, sitting in the cockpit, ordered the cadets to line up, and each in turn start the engine. They were allowed only one chance. At each failure, Oda would descend from the cockpit and slap the cadet across the face. (More loss of face).

One day the young Sasakawa suggested to Oda that he, *Oda,* demonstrate the precise motions needed to start the engine. Oda, in what could only be considered a challenge, to save *his* face, agreed. And he himself failed. He tried again and again but he failed every time.

All the cadets in the unit, who were lined up to watch this demonstration, had a hard time keeping straight faces. This only increased Oda's fury and frustration. Sasakawa smiled at me, remembering the incident.

"Suddenly Oda ordered *me* to start the engine. In those days I was a big show-off. Instead of identifying myself with the plane, as I used to under Nishide's wise guidance, I turned towards the men watching me. I yanked at the propeller and failed to duck away from it as the blade came down."

The result of this episode was a severe wound to his right shoulder. He was rushed to Eriji Hospital in Nagoya, where he was immediately operated on. He still remembers the excruciating pain as the surgeon sawed his shoulder blade so that the damaged bone would knit properly. He claims that he uttered not a single sound, a stoicism which impressed the surgeon and staff. When Dr. Hideshige Sotogaki visited the young patient, he congratulated him on his Samurai like behaviour.

This injury eventually led to his release from the Air Corps. It took a year for the shoulder to mend, part of the treatment being long soaks in hot springs.

Today Sasakawa uses his right arm in a perfectly normal manner, but it is half an inch shorter than this left arm. "If I tell myself, this will hurt, it will. But I tell myself it doesn't, and so it doesn't."

In later years he developed his own personal philosophy about the connection between a man's spiritual beliefs and the body's responses. The mutilated shoulder was just the beginning.

Once Ryoichi's shoulder was mended, he set out on an entirely different course. Gone was the show-off pilot, with his youthful enthusiasms. Now he was a serious young man and something of a hero in his home town.

At that time the village of Toyokawa was apparently run by politicians who could best be described as Rabelaisian roustabouts. All-night drinking parties took place in the village Council Hall; sake was provided by taxpayers' money. More taxpayers' money was spent on the services of geisha girls. In the morning when the business of government was supposed to be taking place, the village chiefs, other officials and various followers were sleeping off hangovers. It was clear that the village chief was trying to consolidate this position using parties and geisha girls.

The villagers were quite well aware of these circumstances, and yet they seemed powerless to effect a change.

When Ryoichi appeared on the scene, he was an ideal candidate

to champion their cause. He had been a member of the élite Army
Air Corps. He was the son of one of Toyokawa's leading and most
respected citizens. He belonged to a family of means. And he already
had his own brand of charm and persuasion.

He was formally approached by a group of citizens and asked to
run for office. He readily agreed. This proved to be a turning point in
his life.

He campaigned with all the energy and determination which had
previously gone into his flying career, and when the election count
was made, he came up with a huge majority of votes. So he became
a councillor for a four-year term when he was just 22 years old.

He at once attacked the problem of the nightly drinking. Since this
was already a public scandal, the other councillors had to admit to it
and vow to change their ways. How was this possible? The young
Sasakawa told them in public that getting drunk was fine "once or
twice a year". It was thoroughly permissible. But getting drunk in the
Council Hall was outrageous. They were using taxpayers' money! It
is characteristic of Ryoichi Sasakawa that he tackled one key problem. In this instance the problem was sake. Once the drinking
stopped, the Village Council got down to business.

Sasakawa says that during his four-year term of office he worked
and accomplished his aims during the first two years. In this short
span of time he reformed the Toyokawa Village Council — a body of
twelve men, all of them his seniors.

On 8 January, 1922 Sasakawa's father died. Ryoichi Sasakawa, at
23, was head of the household, and wholly responsible for his
widowed mother, his brothers and sisters. He was also responsible
for the family's fortune. This turned out, much to his surprise, to be
quite considerable. Tsurukichi Sasakawa, a respectable brewer and
wholesaler of sake whose migrant workers lived right next to his
modest house, had amassed a fortune. This was cleverly diversified
in cash, government bonds, life insurance and other securities.
Obviously, the father, because of his modest way of life, had not
needed to use his wealth, and so had left his oldest son a millionaire.
At the age of 23, this must have been a challenge. He may have
experienced the temptation to squander this inheritance — on
planes, women, houses.

But perhaps because Ryoichi had spent time working for and with his father, he did not waste the money he had inherited. The family continued to live in the same house; the same servants remained with them; their lives remained more or less the same. The only change was the closing of the brewery business which was becoming less successful in the face of competition from the big brewing houses.

When Sasakawa first came into his fortune and having sold the brewery, he started out by just "playing" at making money. But he soon discovered that he had a real talent for commodity trading. To someone unaccustomed to this business, his success story is a lesson that can be viewed with either alarm or amusement. This is what he told me.

"One of my father's friends, Umezo Ikeda, who used to play *go* with him, was a broker who had a rice exchange in Osaka. I thought he could help me, and so one day I went to him with my father's government bonds and cash and other securities, and asked him to keep them for me.

"While I was there I looked at the rice exchange. The whole atmosphere excited me — the fast buying and selling — the urgency of the place. I immediately thought of investing a part of my inheritance. What could be the harm? But Ikeda felt responsible. 'Oh, no! It's far too risky!' Still I wanted to have a little fun, to take a little risk. My father had told me that Ikeda was a cautious man and not always successful in his personal commodity speculations. In spite of Ikeda's warnings I decided to risk a small amount of money on the rice exchange. My theory was that if I did the opposite of what Ikeda was doing, there'd be no risk. I decided to find out when he sold and when he bought. Then I would do the reverse. At my first request to buy, Ikeda was shocked. He insisted that I was throwing away my father's hard-earned money. So, with the utmost respect to both my father and my friend, I said, 'You know how much I honour my father, and you also know how much he has trusted me during his lifetime. . . .' At the mention of my father, he agreed to the transaction.

"During the next few months my whimsical theory paid off. The first two cables from Ikeda informed me that my investments were making money. Occasionally I travelled from Toyokawa to Minoo, and from Minoo to Osaka to see Ikeda, and find out what was happening. Each time Ikeda told me I had made more money. Each time, against his warning, I reinvested the profits. Never once did I touch the principal. And I was well on my way to making my first fortune.

"Eventually, to save Ikeda's feelings, I went to another commodity exchange. Then I only made courtesy calls to old Ikeda. I knew him to be a man of pride, just as my father had been."

Sasakawa went on to make profitable investments in a variety of commodities: rice, sugar, silk threads, and others.

In 1924 he had 40 billion yens worth of assets calculated at today's rates. Typically Sasakawa says: "The secret of making money is not to focus on it, not to be nervous about it, just be relaxed about it. This is why I've come to think there is nothing as easy as making money."

Chapter 5

National Politician and Prisoner

He who smiles
rather than rages
is always the stronger.
(Japanese proverb)

In the 1920s and 1930s Japan was in turmoil. On 1 September, 1923 the great Tokyo Earthquake shook all of Japan. Tokyo, its port of Yokohama and neighbouring cities were levelled by fires. Huge tidal waves and repeated shocks battered the land, leaving some 130,000 people dead. Losses in business and real estate were beyond calculation. And this turbulence of nature was reflected in the turbulence of men's affairs.

There was assassinations, attempted coups, extremists of both left and right gained large followings. In 1925 the Diet passed a bill granting universal male suffrage. This increased the number of voters from three million to 14 million. Politicians lost much of their influence. Throughout this period there was a growth in the power of the army (and to a lesser extent the navy) which was supported by the peasantry against the interests of the city *bourgeoisie* and capitalists.

Poverty and overcrowding bred inevitable tensions among the farmers and peasants. Some 2900 people per square mile of usable farmland made Japan the most overpopulated nation in the world; more than half this population were peasants and fishermen, who together earned less than a fifth of the national income. Tenant farmers were close to starvation, and many peasants were forced to sell their daughters into prostitution to avoid starvation.

This was all happening against a backdrop of the world wide depression of the thirties. International trade, on which Japanese industry depended, was slowly coming to a standstill. The drastic fall in the price of rice and silk hit Japan's rural areas particularly hard. And at the same time, the army was demanding and receiving huge budget allocations.

Amongst all the political turmoil, people throughout the country were getting together in small groups to try and create a new political force. But these groups were scattered. Soon it was clear they needed a leader — a man of courage, with money and political experience.

Sasakawa's personal wealth and secure position did not blind him to Japan's troubles. He was keenly aware of them. He had already given support to one political publication. He had been approached by a man called Fukugatsu Kimura. Kimura was a man of letters who needed financial backing. He asked Sasakawa to be president of his company, Kokubosha (National Defence Company). This company's publication, *Kokubo* (National Defence) needed subsidizing. Sasakawa agreed with its aims: to combat the growing left-wing groups; to protect Japan from what he saw as her enemy within, namely socialism; and to help alleviate the confusion caused by labour unions throughout the country. He put up the money for this monthly publication.

Then in 1931 Sasakawa took on a more active role and formed the *Kokusui Taishuto* or People's Party of the Nation. The three tenets of the People's Party were: (1) love and protect Japan; (2) identify with the feelings of the masses; (3) clean up government politics and eradicate corruption. Sasakawa told me: "These were also my ideals for Japan."

Meanwhile political unrest continued. In 1932 the Prime Minister was gunned down by nine army and navy officers. To all intents and purposes, the military was taking over the government.

Sasakawa told me:

"In such a situation ideals are not enough! There must be a channel between the ruling classes and the working masses. There has to be a solid foundation. There cannot be too much power concentrated at the top or the entire structure of society will topple. A pyramid needs a strong broad base. This is what we needed, and what my People's Party would give the country."

The party had ideals, funds and some brilliant minds at work. Yet the political climate was cloudy and ominous. Soon it was a raging storm. In February 1936 young army officers marched some 1500 troops out of barracks and laid seige to the governmental centre of Tokyo. Officers roamed the city, trying to assassinate the new Prime Minister, and much of the Cabinet. The Prime Minister escaped being killed by hiding under dirty laundry in a closet when the killers came to his home, but others were not so fortunate. After four days of killings, the terror ended as abruptly as it had started, but these ghastly murders did nothing to discredit the military in the eyes of the people or reduce its political power. (From February 1936 to the outbreak of the war, Japanese politicians who blocked any of the army's plans lived in fear of assassination.)

The decline in orderly parliamentary procedure was dramatically evident when party participation in the Cabinet was eliminated under a Prime Minister who was also an army general.

At this time Sasakawa was still active in the field of aviation. He had purchased the land for an airfield just outside Osaka, and had established a school for the training of pilots. In 1932 he formed and headed an organization called the National Aviation Union.

This juxtaposition of roles — politician and aviator — is typical of Sasakawa. The one role enhances the other, and vice versa. For instance, he always drew a big crowd for his People's Party speeches. If there was an airfield near the place of his engagement, he'd fly his own plane in. His landings were dramatic, and added to his prestige.

As president of the People's Party of the Nation, Sasakawa was keenly aware of his responsibility. "My country was in such turmoil. Our economy was suffering from wars abroad and foreign embargoes. Our people were hungry. And we were divided amongst ourselves. The time was ripe for all sorts of rebellion. Assassinations were only a sign. Hunger and poverty were other signs. We were a confused people. I felt I had the custody of precious lives. I felt I had a responsibility that was heavier than the earth itself."

During this time, as one might expect, he made a lot of political enemies. Then rumours of his assassination reached his ears. . . .

One of his enemies was Sango Satake, president of a large railroad company of which Sasakawa was a major stockholder. The power struggle between these two men was both personal and ideological, although it is unclear exactly what specific charges were made by Satake against Sasakawa and his People's Party followers. But Osaka was the scene of a great deal of political agitation and a great many arrests.

"At that time the judicial system in Japan presumed a man's innocence until he was proven guilty. But this was just a theory, just on the books. In reality this theory didn't exist. There were many arrests in Osaka on trumped up charges. . . ."

Sasakawa was in Tokyo when he heard of the arrests of many of his People's Party members. He had also been tipped off, again via rumour, of the immediate possibility of his own arrest and imprisonment. He was familiar with police corruption, and knew that his money would be confiscated. So he thought of an ingenious plan of hiding it. He took his money and various securities out of the bank and travelled to Osaka. This time it was not to visit his old friend Ikeda. It was to hide his fortune where nobody would find it.

That night in Osaka he placed his cash in empty oil drums in the warehouse of his airstrip. He had one confidant, a man by the name of Jugo Kondo to whom he told his plan. Jugo Kundo was to make sure that the barrels which contained the money were to remain on the bottom tier of the petrol supply. Kondo was also to make sure that as each petrol drum was emptied, it was to be immediately replaced. In this way the barrels containing the money on the bottom tier would never be touched. Kondo was a loyal and efficient employee — a rare person in those times of intrigue and counter-intrigue.

Sasakawa's arrest was to be made by Deputy Investigator Honda under orders from Sango Satake, a fact he learned from another loyal friend. This was a woman, the owner of the restaurant and geisha house, Azuma.

This woman knew each guest, who was meeting whom, and what their business was about and she made note of many conversations and monetary transactions.

Apparently Sango Satake used this particular place for his meetings with Honda. Satake needed Honda's help to implement a plot to have Sasakawa arrested. Then Sasakawa would have no power in the railroad company, and his People's Party would be without a leader.

"My friend kept careful records. She knew exactly which man had paid for which geisha girl, and the amount. She also documented the monetary transactions between Satake and Honda."

Sasakawa was well aware of the importance of this documentation, and was grateful to receive it from her. It would be needed for his trial if his arrest ever came about and he found himself in prison.

The following day Sasakawa presented himself to the authorities of the Osaka prison. He vividly remembers the circumstances. It was to be a deal: release of his Party members in exchange for his imprisonment. The result: he was summarily arrested and put into prison. None of his Party members were released. His so-called crimes were "attempted intimidation", "violence", and "interference".

On his arrest, the police began a thorough search of his homes in Tokyo and Osaka, the homes of his relatives and close associates. In all they searched eleven houses. They tore up the *tatami* mats; rifled through *Butsudans*; cut open *futons*, determined to get their hands on his money. The Japanese house is simplicity itself. There are few hiding places. The police found no money. But they found the incriminating documents kept by Sasakawa's restaurant owner friend.

When Sasakawa heard that these papers had been found he told the authorities: "Good. These are important documents. They will be needed for my defence. Save them."

The documents were somehow misplaced, and never recovered.

Sasakawa approached prison with a sense of destiny and spiritual fervour.

"I felt God had put me here for a specific purpose."

He looked around at his fellow prisoners. There were twenty-five to thirty of his own followers. Then there were some doing hard labour. And there were some old men who could do nothing at all. The prison was ill equipped to house so many new prisoners; conditions were unsanitary; food was severely rationed, and yet a population of rats seemed to flourish.

He was no longer in the complex world of politics and business, with their intrigues and treacheries, and he threw his energies into improving prison conditions. He immediately approached the prison authorities and appealed to them on behalf of the sick and the old prisoners. His first successful effort was providing these old men with *yutampos* (tin containers of hot water), thus providing them with a certain degree of warmth day and night. Younger men who were consigned to hard labour all day received their *yutampos* at night. Other reforms which he negotiated were almost as important to the prisoners as physical warmth. These were items for spiritual encouragement, and self-respect. They included small vases with ceremonial flowers, combs and pomade for the hair, and mirrors.

"I looked at this time in prison as a gift from God. I wasn't angry. Some of my followers were, because they were unable to accept their fate. I was cheerful! Of course, there were times when this cheerfulness thoroughly exasperated the prison guards.

"Sometimes my injured right shoulder pained me. This was a reminder to use my spiritual strength to overcome my body's exhaustion. This is how, I believe, it was possible for me to remain warm at night and not need the *yutampo*."

Sasakawa also showed his adaptability in dealing with bedbugs and fleas. Shaking them out of his quilt before going to bed at night, he cocooned himself within the quilt in such a way that they could not reach his body. This made sleep possible.

"Another lesson I learned during these years was how to deal with the abuse of power. I developed my own theory of power with love. This did not happen overnight. It was the slow lesson I was to learn from a small insect."

A small praying mantis took up lodgings in his cell. At first this 3-inch predatory insect was merely one more pest. It zoomed around the cell, and occasionally attacked Sasakawa with its spiny front legs. At first he slapped it away. Then he realized that it has as much right to exist as he did. He decided to make friends with this winged nuisance, and share his food with it. Slowly a relationship developed between man and insect. When Sasakawa received his bowl of rice he would tap his *hashi* (chopsticks) on the bowl, and the praying mantis would descend and eat its morsel. One day the guard observed *his secret forces* of revelation. His celebration of the insect's right to live and the lesson he learned from his friend about love between the powerful and the powerless was the first seed in the global garden of his philanthropy today.

"It is a matter of faith and conviction. Faith speaks to the mind. And the mind speaks to the body."

Sasakawa spent nearly two years in Osaka prison at this time. The lessons he learnt there were to be of value throughout his life.

Chapter 6

War

Despise not an enemy because
he is weak
Fear him not because he is strong
(Isoruku Yamamoto)

Sasakawa got out of prison on 24 July, 1937, although he was not acquitted of his so-called crimes until 26 December, 1938. By the time he regained his freedom, war was already beginning to seem inevitable. Since Japan's emergence from 250 odd years of isolation in 1854, she had been waging wars and winning large areas of land without any substantial setbacks. Her encroachment over Southeast Asia had been steady, and when the League of Nations admonished her for her military actions in Manchuria she simply resigned from the League. Nationalism was very strong at this time and as we have seen the army had to all intents and purposes gained power well before the outbreak of the Second World War.

Japan had taken over Manchuria, Korea, Inner Mongolia and parts of French Indochina almost with ease. Nevertheless, looking with hindsight, it seems surprising that she was so ready to take on the United States. Even by Tokyo's own estimation, the United States had far greater economic and military strength than Japan. Indeed, many Japanese felt that in the long run the United States was likely to win any conflict.

One of the people who held this view was Isoruku Yamamoto who was Admiral and Commander in Chief of Combined Fleet from 1939 until killed in action in 1943. He is quoted as warning the military bluntly: In the first six to twelve months of war with the United States

and Britain, I will run wild and win victory after victory. After that
... I have no expectation of success." He was as good as his word as
he was the architect of the Japanese victory of Pearl Harbour.

Japan's only hope was in a pair of massive and simultaneous surprise attacks, one on the U.S. naval base at Pearl Harbour, the other
on the mainland and offshore islands of Southeast Asia. These
attacks had to be executed with enormous speed so that the United
States war machine did not have time to roll into high gear. The U.S.
fleet, Yamamoto noted, was in port every Saturday and Sunday. In
all, ninety-four vessels were densely clustered in an area not 3 miles
square, with only one channel open to the sea and a single torpedo
net streched across the channel's mouth. It was a "bottle-neck", a glo-
rious target.

The success of his long-shot attack against Pearl Harbour made
Yamamoto an overnight hero in Japan. (Later he was responsible for
Japan's subsequent triumphs throughout the Pacific . . . on Wake
Island, Luzon, Manila, Corregidor, Bataan, the subjugation of the
Philippines . . . until the first U.S. triumph on Midway.) Nevertheless,
Isoruku Yamamoto was against the war. Once it had started, he told
Sasakawa: "We must establish a schedule for the war, so that we can
conclude it within a year. The right time to negotiate with Great Bri-
tain and the United States is when we take Singapore. Then we
should approach Great Britain and the United States and make a
peace treaty. If we go any further, our military leaders will want
Burma, then India. If you take Burma and India from Great Britain,
it's like taking a bedwarmer from an old man." Sasakawa asked him
how long it would be to take Singapore. He said six months. Actually
Japan took Singapore in about two months.

There was quite a bit of support for Yamamoto's views especially
among naval officers.

Unfortunately however, it was General Hideki Tojo, the most pro-
Axis member of the Cabinet, who became simultaneously Prime
Minister of Japan and head of the army. Thus Tojo and his army sup-
porters gained military control over the civil governement. Tojo had
never been outside Japan, unlike the worldly Yamamoto who had
studied at Harvard and had visited pre-war Germany. Tojo's understanding of the world outside Japan was very limited. His war plan

was simply to further Japanese expansion by military means regardless of cost.

Sasakawa's views on the war were very much a reflection of his friend Yamamoto's. He was against war with the United States on the pragmatic grounds that in the end Japan could not win a long war with the United States. I asked him what he did after he heard about Pearl Harbour. He told me: "My first thoughts were . . . what *can* I do? . . . I was against the war, and against the war cabinet. I decided that the best way I could serve my country was to be in a position of power in Parliament."

So Sasakawa once again entered the political arena and fought an election. He told me:

"The campaign was hard and full of heckling. I was known to be critical of the Japanese policy of aggression. And to be against the war with America."

Sasakawa's campaign for election was hampered by the fact that he was not officially endorsed by the *Taisei Yokusankai* (Imperial Rule Assistance Association, a nationalist political association of the war years). Yet in 1942 he and some seventy unendorsed candidates were elected to the House of Representatives.

"Together we formed an informal political group. I was the shadow secretary-general of that group. Of course we had no official name."

Despite Sasakawa's opposition to the war, he was, as he says, a patriot. Like Yamamoto, he in fact worked very hard for the war effort. Whatever their internal differences, the Japanese did feel a strong sense of unity as a nation at this time—a nation united against the rest of the world. Sasakawa was no exception. He told me:

"Once you are at war you must go all the way. You must show determination to go all the way."

He is rather vague about what he in fact did. After he got out of prison in 1937 he set about re-establishing his financial position, something he was able to do because he had managed to protect much of his wealth (as we saw in the last chapter). He made international business contacts and was indirectly involved in trade with China. I tried to find out about his business activities during the war.

I asked him:

"Did you travel abroad at this time?"

"No, I didn't travel abroad but I did go to Korea and China. I went there on business. In Japan there was an acute shortage of wood. It was up to me to implement the important exchange of goods between Korea and China and Japan. My major businesses were in the mining and drilling industries. They were essential to Japan's wartime effort, if not directly for armaments."

Sasakawa's reticence on this and other points concerned with his wartime activities is at least in part due to the general Japanese reluctance to talk about the war. There is even today a feeling of shame about what happened in the war, and the Japanese are still very sensitive about this. But it is clear that ironically, Yamamoto and Sasakawa, two men who felt strongly that the war should not take place, were two of the people who strove hardest for Japanese success.

During the war years Sasakawa lived in Tokio when the Diet was in session. His home was in Shibuya, a residential area near the Meiji Shrine. Whenever possible he returned to his family home in Osaka. Food and other necessities were rationed, and life was difficult, as it had been for some time, but Sasakawa found his mother and sister, Yoshiko, in good health.

I asked him whether he was ever afraid for himself or his family.

"I was never really afraid. I am a fatalist. I always feel that what will happen will happen. It seemed, too, that others shared my feelings. I would say that none of us were afraid. As a fatalist, I felt that God would take care of everything."

Apparently it is characteristic of the Japanese to accept fate without rebellion.

It was during the war that Sasakawa met his wife. Despite the war, performing artists and their various organizations were flourishing in Japan. Japan has a strong traditional theatre—the Kabuki, the Noh, the Bunraku puppet-drama, poem chanting. As a member of the Diet, Sasakawa was Chairman of the Nippon Geinosha (Japan Performing Arts Council). He was appointed to this position for the purpose of unifying the various fields of performing arts under one central organization.

In 1942 Sasakawa met a 19-year-old girl of astonishing beauty. Her name was Shizue Miyakawa. She was a talented soloist at poem chanting. She also played the *biwa* beautifully. This is a traditional kind of lute. Her musical training had begun at the age of 5 and by the age of 9 she was sufficiently professional to have been awarded a teachers certificate to teach the *biwa*.

Sasakawa heard her singing, and thought to himself, as he told us later, "For an amateur, she was the best."

If she was not then a professional singer in Sasakawa's opinion, she was certainly busy. She travelled with a professional group to Manchuria much as American U.S.O. entertainers toured overseas to perform for our troops abroad.

She spoke to us during our visit in Hiratsuka.

"During the war we gave performances at armament factories. In early 1943 we travelled to Manchuria for two months. We were sent by the Department of the Army and travelled in a group. Of course we were closely chaperoned. Otherwise my parents would have never allowed me to do this work.

"I met my husband in 1942. I was 19 at the time. Our first encounter was that of a performer and a man who happened to be head of the Japan Performing Arts Council.

"At that time there was no particular love relationship between my husband and me. Our romance did not begin until early 1944. At that time I was living in Tokyo with my parents and my older sister. Nobody in my family approved of my obvious affection for Ryoichi. He was twenty years older than me, and my parents disapproved of him on that account. They told me I was an impressionable child and warned me against any infatuation with an older man, despite his prominence in the government. My family has always been artistic and musical. What was this politician doing in my life? My sister wondered out loud how I could be attracted to such a stern-looking man.

"As you know, I was not only young but stubborn. I remember the day we looked for a house. It was a day of heavy bombing in Tokyo. This followed a night of many fires. It was hardly an auspicious time to set up housekeeping. We never really had a honeymoon. But eventually we managed to find and furnish our little home. Life was incredibly chaotic and uncertain.

"During another bombing raid our home was so badly bombed that I fled to my sister's home. Ryoichi was away at that time. When he returned and came to find me at my sister's home, that house didn't exist either. He finally found us all sheltered in the local school gymnasium. It was not until after the war that we were able to live together as man and wife."

The total Japanese surrender to the American and Allied forces in the Pacific had a devastating effect on the national Japanese psyche. Perhaps even today national pride has not fully recovered.

(It is difficult for a Westerner to understand the significance for the Japanese of the success of the Olympic Games that were held in Tokyo in 1964.) And of course the physical side-effects of the atomic bombs dropped on Hiroshima and Nagasaki are still being felt today. The Second World War was a crucial turning point for the Japanese. Personally for Sasakawa it was a central turning point in his life and thought.

Chapter 7

Sugamo Prison

Freedom from desire
leads to inward peace. (Lao-Tse)

The *New York Times,* on Tuesday, 4 December, 1945 in an article by
Burton Crane had the following to say about Ryoichi Sasakawa:
"TOKYO, Dec. 3 (U.P.) — At least one of the war criminals on Gen.
Douglas MacArthur's lastest list feels honored that he was to be so
accused. Ryoichi Sasakawa, ultra-nationalist, declared: 'To be
named by the Allied Army as a war criminal is eloquent proof that I
devoted my whole self to the prosecution of the war.' He added that
all those on the list were 'first class Japanese'."

Nine days elapsed between the date he was put on the war criminal list and his actual arrest on 11 December, 1945. During this time
he told his family and friends: "If I am fortunate enough to be designated a Class A war criminal, please don't feel sorry for me. Let us
celebrate! I have passed the exam to go into prison!"

And he was true to these words.

"I entered Sugamo dressed in the traditional *hakama* and *haori*
(the Japanese costume for the most formal occasion). I rode in a car
followed by a brass band on a truck, and five musicians playing
drums. A banner read: 'A Farewell Celebration for Mr. Sasakawa'!"

"Were you escorted by the Occupation Authorities?

"No, I was not. I turned myself in. I had passed the exam!"

One can only guess at the reaction of the Allied authorities and the
American guards and wardens at Sugamo prison. Certainly this performance could hardly have escaped anyone's attention. Some of the
prison staff were amazed at this flamboyant demonstration. Japan

44

had just been beaten to her knees; as a nation her pride and dignity had been stripped from her; her cities had been razed; and her people were starving. Yet *this* prisoner arrived as if he were the victor.

As a Class A war criminal suspect, Sasakawa knew that in all likelihood he would be sentenced to death. Shizue, his wife, was also aware of this possibility. Three days before his actual arrest they posed for a formal photograph.

"I had even prepared a grave for myself."

Yet once again he approached prison with a sense of destiny. He was determined to survive this ordeal, however long it lasted, and transform it into an experience of lasting value. He was here for a God-given reason, and he would make the most of it. He did.

In prison he was instantly recognized as a leader. His cheerful disposition, while it aggravated certain guards, made him popular with his fellow prisoners. He was elected team leader to negotiate on their behalf with the authorities.

"We were close to being starved, and many of us were suffering from malnutrition. At first the Occupation Forces were responsible for the prisoners' food rations. But the American food did not suit the Japanese prisoners, and Japanese food all over the country was severely rationed. So there was very little food to go around. I was elected to negotiate for more food."

Sasakawa's previous prison term was another reason for his leadership.

"I remembered my days in Osaka prison and the importance of keeping up one's strength. I was always careful to eat my rice very slowly and chew it thoroughly. Only then would I touch the soup. Most of the prisoners were so hungry that they poured the soup into the bowl of rice and gulped it down. This is a very unhealthy habit. And it leaves you hungrier than before. Prison is an education in many ways. . . ."

I asked Sasakawa about prison conditions, and his answers led our dialogue in many directions.

"In prison, each cell was the size of two *tatami* mats. One mat for each person.

My philosophy is that it's not the *physical* space to be concerned about, but what's in your heart and mind. Many prisoners suffered because they were used to luxury. They had a hard — if not impossible — time adapting. They couldn't change their minds about their situations. I would tell them: 'Get yourself used to this life. Look, they feed you for free, there's medicine, and there are no thieves because we've got guards all round us'!"

A singular advantage that Sasakawa had at this time was an intuitive knowledge of the American way of interrogation.

"It is very different from the Japanese. Americans want a definite 'Yes' or 'No' answer. The Japanese tend to circle around the answer and take quite a while getting to the point. This may be another reason for my getting along with most of the prison authorities."

I asked Sasakawa about prison conditions. He said that he was never denied food or water, nor was he ever beaten or kicked or hurt with any weapon. He was never put in solitary confinement and when he was ill he received good medical treatment.

"Were you ever denied visits from your family or friends?" I asked. Sasakawa replied:

"I was never denied visits from my wife or members of my family. However the rules for Class A war criminal suspects were very strict. For the first six months no visitors were allowed. Afterwards we were allowed one visitor per month. These visitors had to be listed with the Occupation Authorities, and take their turn. For this reason, I saw my wife as much as possible, and other members of my family deferred to her. I never saw my mother. I saw my younger brother Ryohei once."

Prisoners were not allowed to receive food from outside, but they were allowed letters.

"My mother didn't write to me at all while I was in prison. She had always told me, 'Son, you are in charge of yourself.' My wife wrote to me constantly. Sometimes I was so busy I didn't have time to read her letters. And when I was released from prison I was ashamed to be carrying her unopened letters. She was not upset because our reunion was so beautiful."

Despite the fairly reasonable treatment, in general Sasakawa felt that he personally was noticeably worse treated than other prisoners. He seems to have got on the wrong side of one of the guards, not an American guard but a *nisei* (second generation Japanese American) working for the Occupation Forces in Sugamo.

"His name was Kurihara. He made me clean the shallow sewage trough with a toothbrush, and I had to do it without bending my knees. He did this mostly when everyone else was outdoors having their exercise period, and he ordered me to use my right arm which was the one that still hurts sometimes (that old propeller accident reminding me of my youthful arrogance). Kurihara also ordered me to clean up the room where other prisoners were hung from the scaffold and gallows. Nobody wanted this job. I saw it in a different way. I felt that the people who had passed on had called me to their place of death to pray for them. I never actually witnessed a hanging, but my guard friends told me about it, and I told my cellmates. We were all still under the threat of capital punishment."

Kurihara was not only a sadistic guard to the Japanese, he was also giving the occupation forces a bad name. The politically astute Sasakawa saw his chance and reported the guard to Headquarters, not only on his behalf and those of his cellmates in this high security prison, but on behalf of a particular individual, Eiji Amo, former Deputy Minister in the Ministry of Foreign Affairs. Kurihara had reduced this prisoner's food ration to one piece of bread and one glass of water a day for five days. As a result of this report, Kurihara was transferred elsewhere.

"Of all the guards about 80% were good guys, and about 20% were bad guys."

Sasakawa often received special attention from the good guys, gifts of cigars and chewing gum. "I'll never forget my first experience with chewing gum. I thought it was some sort of candy. I chewed and chewed and chewed, expecting it to dissolve. But nothing happened. Finally, rather shame-faced, I took it out. To this day I cannot appreciate gum-chewing. I suggested to the guard that maybe he could give me chocolate next time."

Meanwhile, outside prison the Japanese nation was having to face up to defeat and to all the problems, such as economic chaos, that came with it. General MacArthur (Supreme Commander for the Allied Powers — usually referred to as SCAP) has been described as an extremely self-willed commander who only took general orders from Washington and none at all from the Allied nations. Yet his cast of mind and character apparently appealed to the Japanese, who needed guidance and leadership to dig themselves out of the rubble. This he was to provide with considerable success, but not without setbacks.

SCAP faced almost insurmountable problems.

Here was a country whose psychic wounds were severe, and whose economy was so critically maimed (if it could be called an economy at all) that it was to take a whole decade before it crept back to the level of the 1930s. Here was a country flooded with Allied troops and shorn of her conquests, which were considerable. All over East Asia and the Pacific Japanese troops and civilians were being rounded up (more than six and a half million of them), and dumped on Japan. Here was a country of great social and political turmoil. Here was a country which, above everything else, had to be demilitarized. Thus Class A war criminal suspects were jailed, and seven men, including General Hideki Tojo and one civilian former Prime Minister, were executed. The Japanese army and navy were completely demobilized, and their ships and weapons destroyed.

Last but perhaps not least, the Japanese *zaibatsu* had to be formally disbanded. The *zaibatsu*, best described as an excessive concentration of wealth or consortium, was considered one of the villains behind Japan's imperialism, which in turn necessitated aggressive foreign policy, not to mention global war.

In prison, under constant surveillance from American guards, Sasakawa was not unaware of these facts. Did his cheerful disposition hide a certain anguish? As we talked together in Hiratsuka, he merely said that in his "spare moments" he tried to think of ways in which he could alleviate the suffering of Japan. And the world.

And in fact this was the most important effect of prison on Sasakawa. It gave him time to reflect on the war that Japan had just been through. As the months dragged on and became years, Sasakawa's views on war and peace changed radically. While he had been against Japanese involvement in the Second World War on pragmatic grounds (it was bad for business and in any case Japan would lose a war with the USA), he had not believed in peace as a goal in itself. Now he came to think that any war in the future — a war with atomic bombs — would mean the end of the world. Gradually he decided that in any time left to him once he emerged from prison he would try to do everything he could to stop war. Up until the war he had been a businessman, a politician and a financial tycoon. Now he vowed that if he survived the ordeal of prison he would devote his life, his prodigious talents, his financial resources and his spiritual strength towards one single goal. It was not a simple one. It was, and still is today, the most complex and illusive goal in the entire history of mankind: world peace. So in Sugamo prison Sasakawa changed from Japanese patriot to world citizen.

How could he start on this path? First of all he wrote to General MacArthur.

"I wrote to General MacArthur many, many times. I wanted a trial in court. I was a Class A war criminal suspect and I wanted my time in court. Then I could express my beliefs. This would be my statement as a Japanese countryman on the absolute necessity for world peace. I wrote to General MacArthur many times, but I received no reply."

In a more practical vein, Sasakawa began to think about how he could work concretely towards world peace. An idea came to him entirely by chance.

One day a prison guard handed Sasakawa a copy of *Life* magazine. Sasakawa could not read English, but he enjoyed the photographs. One photograph made an instant impression on him. It was of a race of small motorboats with outboard engines.

Sasakawa is a man of quick, sudden inspirations, and his thoughts do not necessarily follow a straight line. Yet they usually emerge from a solid factual foundation. He had long been pondering the problem of Japan's dire economic situation, wondering what he himself could do about it — if and when he ever got out of prison.

Post-war Japan, now stripped of her empire, was a small nation consisting of four overcrowded islands. Her great natural asset was water. No part of Japan is more than 70 miles from the sea. What could be done with water? Sasakawa studied the photo of the race and the small American motorboats and felt his inspiration grow.

The day before Christmas Eve, 1948, Sasakawa and other Class A war prisoners were told they would be leaving Sugamo the next day. No reason was given for their release. There had been no trial, no indictments, and no formal procedure of any kind. They were given clothing and transportation to downtown Tokyo.

Shizue was wrapping presents for her relatives and friends. The Japanese also enjoy Christmas, and she had been invited to share Christmas Eve with one of her friends. She was particularly popular on festive occasions because of her ability to play the *biwa*, the traditional Japanese lute, and also to chant traditional Japanese poetry.

Sugamo prison is located also in Tokyo, so when he was released Sasakawa travelled about thirty minutes by tram carrying his few possessions, among them letters from Shizue, and his copy of *Life* magazine.

"I'd been given old U.S. army fatigues to wear that were far too big for me, and a pair of shoes from the Allied Forces. They were also too large. And I had a civilian cap of some sort. I looked really silly. . . ."

He arrived at his home and Shizue's older sister looked up at him in alarm. "She said to me, 'Who are you?' I said, 'I'm Ryoichi Sasakawa!' She didn't even recognize me. When she finally believed me she hurried to fetch my wife. And *she* hardly recognized me!"

Chapter 8

Gambler

Adversity
is the source
of strength
(From *Japanese Proverbs*)

Now he was a free man, what was the 49-year-old Ryoichi Sasakawa
to do?

From 11 December 1945 to 24 December 1948; these 3 years and 14
days had not only changed his physical appearance, but had also
reduced his wordly assets to almost nothing. He had entered Sugamo
prison wearing the traditional robes for ceremonial occasions. He
left it, a small man in cast-off clothes much too large for him.

His reunion with his mother had been very emotional. He had
been twice imprisoned for his political activities, and his elderly
mother begged him to give up politics. It was a solemn promise she
asked of him, but he gave it and has remained true to it. Since that day
he has washed his hands of "ugly political affairs", to use his words.

Politics, then, was an option no longer open to him. But he was
clearly a man with wide vision and a determination to do something
of national and even international importance. He looked around at
war-torn Japan, her economy in such ruins that it would take 10 years
to regain the level of the thirties. Sasakawa felt that to recover and
develop Japan desperately needed world trade. For world trade, she
needed ships. Her entire marine industry had been destroyed and
had still not yet been rebuilt. He said: "I felt Japan's recovery was
completely dependent on shipbuilding. And shipbuilding, as you
know, requires vast sums of money . . . ."

51

Sasakawa needed to find some means of making very large sums of money. Yet he had nothing at all himself and life was very hard for Shizue and him. But as Shizue told me: "My husband had a wonderful idea . . ." This idea had been born in Sugamo, an inspiration from looking at a photograph of a motorboat race.

A Japanese motorboat race is a thrilling spectacle. The boats themselves are something of an engineering marvel. They are graceful in outline and painted in brilliant colours. There are six contestants in each race. Each boat has a number, and so does the driver. Like a jockey the driver is usually small and he has to kneel as he drives the boat. There are 2 minutes in which to jockey for position at the beginning of the race, and then a flying start: deafening sound of outboard motors, sprays of water like silver fireworks, cheers and shrieks from the crowd of spectators. In just 3 minutes it is all over, and the crowd will have to wait another half hour for the next race. Meanwhile there is a rush to the betting windows.

It is, unbelievably, this money from gambling on motorboat racing that has enabled Sasakawa to achieve what he has today—huge loans and subsidies to the Japanese shipbuilding industry, donations to all kinds to a variety of causes within Japan, contributions to good causes throughout the world. It seems ironic that this man, who does not gamble himself, should have dreamt up and brought into being such a popular gambling industry. But popular it is: During the week beginning 3 January 1980 a total of Yen 10,826,527,000 (US dollars 47,072,050) was placed in bets. Total betting from all the twenty-four motorboat racing arenas in Japan brings in approximately 375 million yen every racing day.

The price of admission to an arena in Yen 50 (at today's rates, approximately 25c). The minimum bet is Y200 (under $1), with most people betting a minimum of Y1,000. The fans are for the most part middle-class families, and motorboat racing is a leisure time activity.

The arenas are located on the three southern islands: Honshu, Shikoku, and Kyushu. One arena is built on the Inland Sea. Other arenas are located on rivers and on natural lakes. All arenas are a standard size, and are enclosed wherever they may be situated.

The motorboat racing industry designates a limited number of racing days per month. Generally these are 15 or 16 days. Certain races are famous for their popularity. Large cash prizes are awarded by distinguished citizens such as the Prime Minister of Japan.

The racing drivers are heroes in what is now a highly respected sport. They go through rigorous training in official training centres. Laws regarding drinking and smoking are obvious. But for a specified number of hours before each racing day the drivers are kept in isolation, and cannot be in touch with the outside world. In this way the motorboat racing industry tries to prevent any illegal outside interference.

Of course this industry did not blossom overnight and Sasakawa had a long period of hard work and difficulty in the fifties before his project really began to take off financially. It is interesting to ask how exactly he did get this very successful business started.

It began with vision and foresight, and perhaps an understanding of the mood of the Japanese people after the war. They needed recreation. If they wanted to gamble they could do so on horse, cycle and car races—all of which were popular. There were also a variety of indoor gambling places, but Sasakawa particularly disapproved of these as he felt and still feels they are unhealthy for mind and body. Gambling, he thought, should be an outdoor activity, though certainly some of his critics in Japan today are sceptical about the "healthful" nature of betting on motorboat racing.

Once he had conceived his idea, there were innumerable political, ideological and economic stumbling blocks, apparent dead ends and barriers, and obstacles which seemed insurmountable, along the path to his goal.

Sasakawa, once a prominent financier, was no longer a member of the establishment, that élite of businessmen and politicians and men of military prestige who had previously determined much of Japan's course. Now he was a Class A war criminal suspect, and as such he was a social outcast. He had entered Sugamo prison with his brass band and drummers, a brave gesture, but times had changed and now he had a deep stain on his character—a stigma.

In practical terms, Sasakawa, as an ex-Diet member, and also as a Class A war criminal suspect, was not allowed to set foot in the Diet. Yet he needed the Diet to approve his plan to start this gambling industry. Furthermore, Sasakawa could not allow his name to appear as head of this organization he was about to form. He approached a colleague, Tadashi Adachi, leader of the Japanese Chamber of Commerce, and asked him to become the official head of this project. Tadashi Adachi agreed.

In 1951, Japanese major parties were three—Liberal, National Democratic and Socialist, although it was true that some powerful members of the Diet in those three parties were violently opposed to Sasakawa's idea. How was he to get this controversial bill passed through the various governmental bodies? Here Sasakawa clearly faced another formidable obstacle.

"This bill passed the House of Representatives and was brought to the House of Councillors. Here there were two stages of voting. First by the Transportation Committee; and then by a vote at the General Session. The Transportation Committee passed it; the General Session voted against it. Then, through one of my friends in the Diet, I discovered a little-known regulation of the constitution. It stated that if a bill passed the Transportation Committee, but was rejected by the General Session, such a bill could be brought back to the Lower House again. If it passed there a second time, it was a matter of record and became law."

This is what happened.

Another problem was that life in Japan was still completely regulated and controlled by the Allies under SCAP. This control was particularly visible in the investigation of Japanese in industries, possible concentrations of wealth, or *zaibatsu*. SCAP considered large industries dangerous for obvious reasons; SCAP also considered wealth a threat to the development of a new, democratic Japan. Sasakawa's gambling enterprise on this huge scale was bound to be investigated in detail.

Then there were practical design problems. In prison Sasakawa had already learned a great deal about motorboats from a cellmate, ex-Admiral Soyomu Toyoda, who had learned about motorboat engineering in the Philippines. From these discussions, Sasakawa knew that a special design was needed to create a motorboat suitable for racing in Japan. He felt certain specifications had to be met. The boat should be designed with an outboard engine; it should be as light as possible; finally it should be small, so small that it could accommodate only a single racer, kneeling. He needed a new, original design. He followed this goal with undiminshed energy and influence in various fields until this motorboat became a reality. Today it is the famous Yamato engine and design.

Political adversaries and legal snarls and engineering problems were relatively small forerunners to the giant financial lion in his path. Sasakawa's personal fortune had vanished during the war and without large investments there would be no funds to launch this long-range project which included the design and manufacture of the racing boats, construction of racing arenas, and the necessary franchises for them throughout Japan, spectator grandstands, betting facilities, and the administration necessary to control this sport in an absolutely legal way.

Sasakawa appealed to both his brothers for funds during these years. "My brother, Shunji, was constantly complaining. One day he said, 'Are you trying to make me go bankrupt?' They did, however, help me again and again. But it took a long time to get it all to work."

"These were hard times", Shizue told me. "We had no money but a big idea. My husband and I were very close. I was his secretary. Every day there was some new problem . . . ."

Despite all these enormous obstacles—social, political, financial—the first motorboat race took place on 6 April 1954, just five years after Sasakawa's release from prison. If it did succeed, if it was to grow, motorboat racing at the start was entirely dependant on the magnetism and enthusiasm of one man. No one knew if the crowds would remain faithful to horse, cycle and car racing, or if they would turn to a new sport. Sasakawa managed to keep those around him convinced of the validity and future worth of his new enterprise. He had will power, perseverance, and optimism, traits necessary to keep the industry alive during times of financial failure, political opposition and natural disasters of which Japan has always had more than her fair share. And in five years since his emergence from prison, he had accomplished his first ambition: the creation of an industry with a potential for producing tremendous revenue.

One of the most famous of motorboat racing arenas is the Suminoe Arena in Osaka, and its sponsors are the Osaka Prefecture City Motorboat Racing Union and Minoo City. It is the largest arena in terms of sales of tickets. Its average per day is Y827,960,861 ($3,599,829). Approximately 32,000 fans attend each day.

Mayor Buhei Nakai of Minoo City has quite a bit to say about the old days before the present extraordinary betting figures. According to him; "Once Sasakawa opened the enterprise it was always in the red. There were two opposing factions in the City Council. One group wanted to scrap the plan, and one supported its continuation. Sasakawa said it would be good for Minoo City. He was so sure that he told the Council he would pay the city if it incurred losses. In the case of profits from this industry, such gains would belong to Minoo City. When it came to a vote as to whether or not to continue the races, the motion was carried by one vote."

Today, Osaka Prefecture is the wealthiest in Japan, and this is in large part due to the money it receives from the motorboat racing industry. The people of Minoo City acknowledged Sasakawa's contribution to their city. On 1 August 1962 he was made an honorary citizen.

Prominently displayed in the mayor's office is a large framed calligraphy in Sasakawa's own hand proclaiming his motto. This calligraphy, approximately 4 feet square, hangs on the wall above the mayor's desk, and is a permanent fixture of this important office. In my interview with Buhei Nakai, he said: "This is one of our proudest possessions. Mr. Sasakawa not only believes his own words, he puts them into practice."

The total amount that Sasakawa invested in his idea for motorboat racing was Y5,000,000,000. According to Sasakawa, today this investment has reaped a cumulative *profit* of Y1,904,800,000,000! At the rate of exchange of Y255 to the dollar, this is approximately 7,469,803,900 US dollars.

How is this profit channelled to the sponsoring city and to the different beneficiaries of Sasakawa's philanthropy?

The fans win about 75% of the gross total take from motorboat racing. The remainder is split—all but 2-3%—between the sponsoring city and the regional Motorboat Racing Association which handles payment to the arena itself and covers all operating expenses. It is the remaining 2-3% of the gross total take which is used by Sasakawa for public works and philanthropy.

Under a monopoly agreement with the Transport Ministry, which officially controls motorboat racing, the Japan Shipbuilding Industry Foundation receives this 2-3%. JSIF was a creation of Sasakawa's. He first organized the eighteen separate prefectural motorboat racing associations and then coordinated them into one central administrative body—the Federation of Prefectural Associations of Motorboat Racing. Already by 1955 he was President of this body. Under his guidance, the surplus income accruing to the Association was channelled through their promotion section into support for the shipbuilding industry and social welfare projects. The amount of money available was eventually so large that in 1962 the promotion section was hived off into a completely separate organization—the Japan Shipbuilding Industry Foundation, which is entirely concerned with the giving of donations and subsidies.

Sasakawa is head of the Federation of Prefectural Associations of Motorboat Racing and of JSIF. Thus he has a good deal of control of the popular sport of motorboat racing and of the way its profits are given away. Thus Sasakawa has created and acquired for himself an enormous amount of power and influence in Japan. This power in the hands of one man makes some Japanese critics very uneasy. Nevertheless, Sasakawa is certainly using his power for very worthy ends overseas as he gives away vast sums as his contribution to world peace.

Chapter 9

The Interests of a Philanthropist

Children, come on out:
Clattering along the lane
See . . . It's hailing pearls
(Basho)

Sasakawa has given money to many good causes in his life, and the ones he chooses, as we might expect, are ones in which he has a particular interest. We look in detail at his interest in the United Nations in the next chapter. In this chapter we look at how his interests in the sea, in young people, in peace, in the future, have found expression in gifts to particular projects.

Sasakawa's affinity with water, as shown in his waterology (see Chapter 2), extends to an interest in all things maritime.

"I have always had an inborn longing for the sea, and the romanticism of the sea is still alive in my heart."

His help to maritime projects is not limited to the vast subsidies and loans the Japan Shipbuilding Industry Foundation gives each year for the development of shipbuilding technology. In 1963, Sasakawa decided to do something about his "romanticism" and to do it for the young people of Japan who would be her future.

Inspiration was not long in coming. He would build a maritime museum, devoted wholly to the sea and ships. It would be a unique museum, unlike any other museum in the world. It would be a dramatic, bold statement of Japan's emergence as one of the world's foremost maritime nations. And it would look to the future. It would be called the Museum of Maritime Science.

Meanwhile the distance between inspiration and realization was immense. The project would go through many stages, requiring huge sums of money and the mutual co-operation of a huge team of experts. These included a six-member mission which went to Europe to conduct research on major museums; planning and approval by the Minister of Transportation; and over seventy specialists to prepare the basic design. This is to list only a few of the experts needed for this project. A site had to be chosen. Ideally it would be some 46,000 square metres near Tokyo Bay. In December of 1969 this site was deeded by the Tokyo Metropolitan Government. One year later construction work started.

On 20 July, 1974 the Museum of Maritime Science was completed and opened to the public. It is built in the shape of a 60,000-ton passenger liner. Its unique appearance, with its 90-metre observation tower, has become a symbol of Tokyo Bay. It stands as the first structure of its kind, not only in Japan, but in the entire world.

Here at the Museum everything about the sea and ships is displayed through actual objects, models and panels to introduce visitors to the maritime world. The emphasis in on the future. In the ratio of displays, 20% of the items are from the past; 30% are contemporary items, and the remaining 50% items for the future.

"I want to widen the dreams of our young people in relation to the history of the sea and ships. I want them to know about maritime science and ocean development and realize their responsibility to build a new future."

On the first day of our visit to Japan, we only had a glimpse of Sasakawa in his Maritime Museum office. I could have spent at least a day wandering around this Museum with the knowledge that I could come back again and again. This "ship" is equipped with many of the features of a real ship. It has a simulated navigation corner, a simulated bridge, a "Captain for a day" corner for simulated navigation. Here visitors can enjoy "steering"; and they can study a variety of navigation equipment, international signal flags, and marine traffic control systems.

Models displayed include submarine oil field excavation devices, under-sea stations, deep-sea work vessels for the observation of marine life, under-sea tunnels, seadromes and marine cities.

Sasakawa believes that in the not too distant future people will be living beneath the sea. In 1971, when he was 72 years old, he put on an aqualung and diving suit to enter the seabed house 8 metres below the surface. He was photographed inside the seabed house talking over the telephone to Prime Minister Eisaku Sato. Sasakawa is now the honorary Mayor of the first seabottom village, anticipating future seabottom development.

Sasakawa's interest in the sea extends to a lively concern for marine safety. One of the major marine safety projects that Sasakawa has helped fund through the Japan Shipbuilding Industry Foundation is the Straits of the Malacca Council. This was set up in April 1969. The Malacca-Singapore Straits are considered an extremely perilous area for marine navigation, and rank in difficulty with the Straits of Dover and the famous Straits of Gibraltar. Many Japanese merchant ships go through these straits because it is the route for the large tankers bringing petroleum from the Middle East to Japan. A marine pollution incident occurred in 1976 when the tanker *Showa Maru* went aground in waters off Singapore, releasing a large volume of petroleum into the sea. This caused great damage to the nations with shorelines on the Straits.

Sasakawa had realized some time before that this incident was bound to happen sooner or later. When he formed the Straits of Malacca Council, he suggested to President Suharto of Indonesia that more lights be provided for the world shipping that passes through these Straits.

Today the activities of the Council cover every effort designed to provide and maintain safety for shipping at sea, including hydrographical surveys, the drawing of charts, and the construction and installation of light beacons and lighthouses. The hydrographic surveys conducted since this disaster showed a shocking number of shallows — almost one hundred. Needless to say, these shallows are fearful navigational hazards. Today four lighthouses, nine beacons, and three light buoys have been installed. In addition, oil spill recovery vessels and buoy-laying vessels have been made available for use when needed.

Sasakawa's greatest interest at the moment is his Blue Sea and Green Land (B & G) Foundation. Although this is not exclusively maritime, like many of his other concerns it has a strong marine element. It was established in June 1973, and is devoted exclusively to boys and girls from the age of ten through their early twenties.

"I worry about our young people today. Our children live in a world of increasing pollution and overwhelming materialism. None of this is good. There is also a great undermining of our rich traditional spirit of Japan. I want to help our children develop healthy minds and bodies. B & G recreation centres provide facilities for many sports such as swimming, tennis, volleyball and fencing. The two major B & G centres are in Tokyo and on Okinawa, and there are forty-five local Marine Centres spread throughout Japan. The facilities would be useless if there were no expert trainers and so we train individuals to train the young people. The B & G Foundation includes an extensive network of highly skilled men and women who have undergone rigorous disciplined training for three months at our training institutes. B & G leaders also serve the communities in which they are stationed."

As a gift for junior and senior high school students and young workers, the Foundation has been running training cruises employing 10,000-ton passenger ships twice yearly for the past two years on the Japan-Philippines-Hong Kong and Japan-Guam-Saipan routes. These cruises were designed to enable young people to experience the wonders of the sea and also to give them a broad outlook extending beyond the boundaries of Japan.

Sasakawa has a deep belief in the ability of young people around the world to experience mutual understanding and friendship. One must give them the opportunity. The physical contact and the sharing of experiences and the friendship and understanding are the seeds of peace to be nourished to create a peaceful world. Part of Sasakawa's *on* includes his sense of duty to provide such opportunities for young people.

When the Okinawa Expo was opened in July of 1975, Sasakawa saw one such perfect opportunity. He convened a World Youth Ocean Assembly centred around the Expo. Approximately one thousand young people from forty-eight nations around the world participated in this event. It was the scene of tremendous sharing through many different forms of marine recreation, including yachting, motorboating and swimming.

"I believe sports is a means of communicating in international society."

Another Exposition for young people and for anyone interested in the future was the Space Science Exposition, which opened on 15 July, 1978 for six months. Again this was the manifestation of one of Sasakawa's dreams. And again it was unprecedented in the world. It was centred around the Museum of Maritime Science in Tokyo Bay.

"Space is unknown. Almost three and a half decades have elapsed since the end of the war. But the world has yet to see true peace. In order to make this world of ours one of richness and abundance, it is essential that the youth of today open their eyes to the new frontiers of space. Space! The hopes and dreams of mankind!" This was the main theme of the Space Science Exposition.

On display was an array of invaluable space development equipment. A major attraction was a real Saturn 1 B rocket never before taken outside the United States, and so large it had to be displayed outdoors. Other objects dramatizing man's exploration of space included an Apollo command ship, a return capsule, and moon rocks. Crowds were particularly thrilled by the "Apollo Theatre" which re-enacted man's first landing on the moon by the Apollo 11 team on 20 July, 1969.

The success of the exhibition was not lost on the Japanese Government and it was reopened from 24 March 1979 to 2 September, 1979. The total attendance at the Space Science Exposition was nearly twelve million, the majority of whom were children.

Sasakawa told me that there were several reasons for creating the Space Expo.

"Japan lags far behind other countries in the field of space exploration. Japan has excellent technological know-how and brilliant scientists. What we lack is a sufficient government budget for space exploration programmes. The unavailability of research and development funds is the biggest bottleneck."

Sasakawa hoped that the Space Expo would be a unique opportunity to have the political, bureaucratic, and business worlds, not to mention ordinary citizens and young people, think of the significance of space exploration.

"It was also held as part of a continuing programme to educate the younger generation."

Sasakawa also hoped that a firsthand examination of many artifacts that had actually been used in space would excite young people about this field of science.

"They will come to realize more clearly that our blue planet is but one small part of the universe. My understanding is that space is the common property of mankind and should be explored for the well-being of the human race...."

Most of the items on display had been sent by the United States National Aeronautics and Space Administration (NASA) and the Smithsonian Institution.

"I deeply appreciated the United States government for its co-operation in opening the world's first space exposition under the sponsorship of my Foundation."

United States Apollo lunar module pilot Eugene A. Cernan joined Sasakawa for the opening of this important event. Here, under one roof, the American envoy and the Japanese philanthropist shared the same view of this globe as seen from space: home for all mankind.

In 1975 Sasakawa became President of the Japan Science Society, and immediately became involved in one of mankind's most urgent problems: the production of suitable foods for the world's growing population.

The Biology Research Committee of the Japan Science Society is carrying out investigations into the utilization and cultivation of the taro plant — a member of the arum family with an edible, starchy tuberous rootstock. The taro has been an important food for people in the tropics for thousands of years. It is believed to have originated in the Indian subcontinent and to have spread from there to Africa and the Americas. When man began to cultivate grains such as rice, barley and wheat more actively, the taro became a less favoured food.

The Biology Research Committee has sent members of its research team throughout Southeast Asia to gather information about taro cultivation and utilization. Field tests on different varieties have also been run. These investigations have produced some important discoveries. Firstly, the taro can be cultivated in regions where the soil is chiefly volcanic ash and thus highly permeable to water. Secondly, the taro can be cultivated with very simple primitive tools. Thirdly, the taro can be grown on slopes where other grain crops will not survive. Thus the taro has the potential to be a very important food resource in times of unstable food supply. The Biology Research Committee of the Japan Science Society is committed to the reintroduction of improved taro plants as an important contribution to mankind's struggle to make more food available.

Sasakawa has another plan for food production. It is to restock the oceans of the world.

Just as the Biology Research Committee has investigated upgrading taros, it has also begun to study methods for the cultivation of tuna fish for human consumption. Many people in the world will grow increasingly dependent upon fish as a source of animal protein. We face a serious problem when the grains that are fed to cattle and other livestock compete with grains grown for human consumption, or when fish fed to other fish are equally desired by humans as a food source.

It is Sasakawa's conviction that the fishing countries—Japan in particular—are robbing the seas. Japan relies heavily on her fishing industry for this staple food. Such fishing has resulted in the tragic loss of many species of fish all over the world—caught by mistake in the fishermen's nets. Sasakawa, like many other ecologists, is outraged by this practice.

"Japan is rightfully criticized for her fishing piracy. Our oceans are steadily being depleted of edible fish. We do not do this with our land. Farmers fertilize the soil and cultivate the crops. Fields are replanted every year, otherwise nothing would grow. We should do this with the oceans.

"I learned that tuna—which we Japanese consume in great quantity— is a species of fish which is both high in protein, and which can also adapt to different ocean environments."

As an ocean fish, tuna have fixed spawning places. Once located, fertilized eggs of newly hatched fish (fry) must be quickly transported to the location where they will be cultivated. While there has been some success with the transportation of fertilized eggs, there has been little experience moving recently hatched fry.

The tuna cultivation research programme of the Biology Research Committee has several experimental activities. In Tahiti, one atoll was chosen as the site for raising fish hatched from eggs. Similar studies of tuna spawning activities off Sicily and Taiwan are also being conducted. Sasakawa hopes to have these tuna cultivation projects underway by the end of 1980.

In one way or another, Sasakawa manages to build cultural bridges a great deal of the time, and in many different ways.

One recent and dramatic example is "Emily". Outside the Maritime Science Museum which we visited there is a specially enclosed area containing the dismantled parts of a Japanese fighter seaplane. Officially designated as Kawanishi H8K2 flying boats all of the Japanese-built Emilys had been destroyed during the war except one—the one we were looking at.

After years of active war service, this Emily was taken by the U.S. Navy. Finally this lone survivor was brought to the United States for testing, was almost scrapped, and then was kept at Norfolk Naval Air Station, Virginia. Here she remained for more than thirty years.

For some time the U.S. Navy had considered returning Emily to Japan, but there were legal and monetary problems. Public law required that the recipient be a non-profit museum operated and maintained solely for educational purposes. Also, the donation had to be made at no cost to the Navy. In 1979 such an organization was found: the Museum of Maritime Science. Here she is now being restored.

Sasakawa said that the Emily's return to Japan is a "kind of combination Christmas and birthday present all wrapped in one".

Chapter 10

United Nations

The moon is a good neighbour
and Mars a distant relative.
(Ryoichi Sasakawa)

Sasakawa entered the field of international philanthropy in a way that is uniquely Japanese. The Japanese philosophy of *on* can best be described as a system of "obligation". This is very different from the Western meaning of the word. For the Japanese, *on* is a virtue to be maintained throughout one's life. Thus, when one incurs an "obligation" or an *on*, repayment of it is almost a never-ending responsibility.

Sasakawa explained this to me in his own words.

"After the war many prominent people and the American government extended a helping hand to us to reconstruct our country. During those hard times certain American philanthropists helped us. It would be rude for us to repay these people themselves, so I found other forms of payment. One of the reasons I must live until I'm two hundred years old is to repay this *on*. Once Japan recovered from the war we were in a position to repay this *on*. One way is to contribute to other countries according to their needs."

This philosophy of *on* has taken Sasakawa around the world many times, and has involved him in projects ranging from the World Youth Ocean Assembly to a gift to New York City of cherry trees in Central Park.

This *on* falls on everyone both great and small. So Sasakawa says: "We must all serve the interests of *all* humanity. The rich with their

66

fortunes, the resourceful with their abilities, and the workers with their strength . . . ."

I asked Sasakawa how much money he had donated through the years for international philanthropic causes. His answer was Yen 17,217,000,000 (US dollars 35,284,340). But generous as this is, his interest extends beyond the mere handing out of largesse, to the problems themselves: How many people can inhabit this earth? What are the earth's resources and what are their limitations? How can we, as one family of many nations, survive? Sasakawa is trying to help answer some of these questions, and to alleviate the suffering of *all* of the peoples of the earth.

Sasakawa first became involved with the works of the United Nations about sixteen years ago when U Thant was Secretary-General. It was then that he realized that the aims and objectives of the United Nations were the same as his own. He has criticisms of it, however. He says:

"I support the U.N. wholeheartedly. But here in the most important international body working for peace, the delegates always give priority to the interests of their own countries . . . . I believe the U.N. should have *world* representatives instead of representatives from individual countries . . . . These people would not be representatives of their respective countries but members of the one-family world . . . . They would be spokesmen for the brotherhood of man."

Reading this, it is easy to imagine that Sasakawa himself would like to be one of these world representatives. As this was not possible, Sasakawa considered just what he could do to help the work of the U.N. agencies that were working to alleviate the suffering of people all around the world. He knew that "a big fire could be started by a single match". As an individual and as President of the Japan Shipbuilding Industry Foundation he could be a "match". So JSIF started giving donations to various U.N. bodies. Over the years these allocations have been far too numerous to detail here. Sasakawa himself feels that his contributions to the World Health Organization (WHO) are of prime importance. Later in this chapter we look in detail at three WHO project areas that he has funded substantially.

But we must mention briefly some other programmes in which Sasakawa has been notably active. Sasakawa is concerned with the

United Nations International Children's Emergency Fund (UNI-CEF), the organization that lends a helping hand to needy children throughout the world. Sasakawa organized a mission to visit facilities in Asian countries. He assumed leadership of the mission himself. In May 1976 the team surveyed UNICEF activities in countries such as Indonesia and Bangladesh, and also conducted meticulous studies on the tragic plight of many children in Southeast Asia. He also assisted with the construction of water projects in Indonesia and Lebanon.

The United Nations Education, Scientific and Cultural Organiza-tion (UNESCO) has also been the recipient of donations for their World Assembly of UNESCO Clubs. Obviously public information is essential to any programme, and so Sasakawa channelled funds to the United Nations World Newspaper Supplement Project to pro-mote understanding for the concept of the New International Econ-omic Order.

In September 1974, when the Japanese government agencies were still skeptical about the refugee issue, JSIF provided the United Nations with sufficient funds to assist its refugee relief activities. Since 1977, it has donated $1,200,000 to the Office of the United Nations High Commissioner for Refugees. During that same time, it has contributed a total of $390,000 to the United Nations Relief and Works Agency.

A typical example of Sasakawa's initiative is a proposition he made at the UNESCO Peace Forum in Paris in November of 1979. He pro-posed to establish a Peace Education Prize. He offered one million dollars toward this programme.

"We must promote peace education. And one cannot do this by mere words. One needs an example from a single individual, and one needs 'bait'. If such an annual prize were awarded, the world would have more peace education programmes."

Sasakawa is that individual, and this first million dollars is the bait.

At this November meeting Sasakawa's proposal was greeted with enthusiastic applause. Representatives of only fifty countries attended this conference, but Sasakawa feels it was a start. This pro-posal is slated to be on the agenda for a UNESCO conference soon.

Sasakawa readily admits to opposition to some of his programmes.

This only makes him redouble his efforts.

"I thrive on opposition", he says.

The three WHO projects which Sasakawa helps fund and which we are going to look at in detail are: the containment of leprosy, the eradication of smallpox, and population control.

Sasakawa's own childhood experiences are the original sources for his interest in two of mankind's most devastating diseases. They are leprosy and smallpox. The most mysterious of these diseases from biblical times to today is leprosy.

"I was about 14 years old when I first became aware that there were lepers in my village. I learned about it from my mother. One day I asked her about a beautiful girl in our village who was not married. My mother said there was someone in her family who was a leper. This girl was not a leper herself, but despite this fact no man would ever marry her. In those days the villagers thought leprosy was both inherited and contagious. This girl was in every sense of the word an 'untouchable'. There were other lepers in our village whom I saw at the temple. When you pray you bring your hands together and your fingers touch each other. These people had no fingers so they prayed with what was left of their hands—small strange stumps at the end of their wrists."

Sasakawa told me:

'One of the most tragic things about leprosy—even today—is that many people still do not consider it a disease. Many people feel that lepers are lepers because their ancestors have commited grievous sins. Leprosy is their punishment for these sins. This is why so many people feel that lepers don't need to be treated. They feel they *can't* be treated. I want to do away with this myth."

Leprosy is a chronic infectious disease caused by a specific micro-organism, *Mycobacterium leprae (Baccilus lepra)* which produces lesions in the skin, mucuous membranes and peripheral nerves. *Baccilus lepra* is airborne. It damages motor nerves and causes paralysis. It produces scarring, swelling, and disfigurement of the body, crippling of hands and feet, loss of feeling in affected areas, and blindness.

The following table shows the number of people who suffer from leprosy in different parts of the world. The figures are from WHO and they are at best only an educated guess due to poor record keeping and other problems in many parts of the world.

Asia and India	6,475,000
Africa	3,868,000
South America	358,000
Oceania	33,000
Europe	52,000
United States	2,000

WHO estimates that only 25–33% of the world's patients are receiving regular treatment.

Whether there is a cure for leprosy or not is a much disputed issue. Dr Yo Yuasa, Medical Director of the Sasakawa Memorial Health Foundation, told me:

"Leprosy is a steadily degenerative disease. However, it can be arrested to the point where there is no pathological process going on. I do not believe it can be totally eradicated. It is unique in many ways. One factor is its long indeterminate period of incubation. Another is that early diagnosis is virtually impossible."

Nevertheless, great strides have been made in the treatment of lepers. Leprosariums in many parts of the world have now replaced the cruel and fearful isolation lepers suffered in the past. (And indeed, good leprosy programmes have often been the beginning of comprehensive medical care projects in which not only leprosy but many other diseases are treated.)

The history of leprosy in Japan illustrates what can be done to contain the disease. In Japan, at the turn of the century, a survey carried out by the Japanese Government found about 30,000 lepers, most of whom were not under regular treatment. Today leprosy in Japan can be considered, if not completely eradicated, at least stabilized with no threat of proliferation. This is due to advances in the medical system of treatment and medical science such as chemotherapy, and to the Leprosy Prevention Laws of 1907 and 1953 which provided measures against the proliferation of leprosy and an integrated system of treatment.

According to Dr. Yuasa; "If Japan's experience and her technology could be put to use in other Asian nations where there is still a high incidence of leprosy, the degree of suffering would be greatly lessened. In many cases leprosy would be arrested."

Dr. Yuasa has worked with lepers for over twenty years. I asked him why he had never contracted the disease. His answer was astonishingly simple. "Approximately 90% of any population has a built-in immunity to the *Baccilus lepra.*"

For Sasakawa the ultimate goal is quite simply the control of leprosy throughout the world. It was for this purpose that he inaugurated the Sasakawa Memorial Health Foundation in May 1974. This Foundation serves as a clearinghouse for many health specialists who contribute their expertise to solving a multitude of health problems in Asia. The faculty of the Foundation became internationally recognized as an authoritative body just after the Foundation's establishment. Since its inception, Sasakawa has arranged for large sums of money for the relief and rehabilitation of leprosy patients throughout the world.

The first leprosarium that Sasakawa built is in Agra, India.

"In my youth I saw lepers and I remember their praying hands. Today when I go to India to visit the leprosarium in Agra, I spend some time there. I meet with the lepers in groups and we joke together. We are human beings together and enjoy each other's company. In this way they sense their humanity and are no longer set apart. I never wear gloves when I touch their deformed limbs. Many people do not know that beyond a certain point leprosy is not contagious. I want to show them that it is a disease, and not a punishment for some unknown sin by some unknown ancestor."

The Sasakawa Memorial Health Foundation called on WHO and the International Federation of Anti-Leprosy Associations to convene the Seminars on Leprosy Control Co-operation in Asia in Tokyo in 1974 and 1975. It also convened the First International Workshop of Training of Leprosy Workers in Asia in Bangkok in November 1976, and the First International Workshop on Chemotherapy of Leprosy in Asia in Manilla in January 1977. These conventions were to discuss the eradication of leprosy from an international standpoint. These meetings were important events in the history of leprosy relief.

The ideas and conclusions of these conferences have been put into action. The Foundation has continued to dispatch and train medical experts to countries that need assistance. Sasakawa states: "We are providing not only material assistance, but also indirect support. The countries concerned, ultimately will have to establish the administrative structures by which they can solve these problems for themselves. I think it is vitally essential for them to train personnel for that purpose."

The second WHO project with which Sasakawa is concerned and which we look at in detail here is perhaps the best known of the three projects we consider.

The announcement of the final eradication of smallpox in the world is a truly epochal event of international importance that dramatically demonstrates Sasakawa's belief in the collective action of nations working together.

Smallpox destroys the skin and quickly kills. It is also a highly communicable disease. One person can be responsible for an almost instant outbreak of smallpox.

Africa was the last continent to suffer from this disease. In Ethiopia the problems for WHO field workers were complicated by many additional factors. Roads were few, and half the population lived more than a day's walk from any accessible road; there was also civil war and famine. Nevertheless, WHO workers trekked for miles across hilly terrain, marshy swamps and managed to cross ferryless rivers in order to reach some villages. Here they were able to recruit and train village residents to serve as surveillance workers and vaccinators. Later, transportation was provided, including helicopters. On 9 August 1976 smallpox ended in that country.

Unfortunately one man escaped the net of the WHO field workers and turned up in neighbouring Somalia. Here nomads disseminated the disease throughout the southern part of the country. In May 1977 a national emergency was declared; additional staff were recruited and special assistance was provided by WHO.

When Sasakawa learned of this situation he increased his support of WHO. Intensive surveillance-containment and vaccination programmes continued, with increasing co-operation and success.

On 8 May, 1980 WHO announced the *total eradication of smallpox from the globe*. It was proclaimed in a ceremonial session at WHO headquarters in Geneva. Secretary-General Halfdan Mahler said the essential elements to this success included "science, technology, political leadership, managerial competence, applied common sense and international support in cash and in kind".

The third WHO project which we consider in detail here has been of interest to Sasakawa for nearly twenty years. In the early 1960s Sasakawa and many others began to think that one of the most important ways to avoid war was to control the world population.

The resources of the earth are limited and unequally distributed among countries, and this is why the population issue has become one of the most urgent problems of mankind.

The population growth rate is alarming because "the world took 1,650 years to double its population from 250 million to 500 million . . . but it took only 15 years to increase the world total from 3,000 million in 1961 to 4,000 million in 1976". The increase rate is highest among the developing countries of South Asia, Africa and Latin America.

In 1967 General William H. Draper, Jr., in the capacity of financial advisor to the United Nations Fund for Population Activities (UNFPA), visited Japan and called on its political and financial circles for international co-operation on this population problem. Six years later General Draper died. In 1975 the Draper Population Fund was established by Mrs. Robin Chandler Duke. Sasakawa donated a large amount of money from the Japan Shipbuilding Industry to the U.N. programme in this field through the Japanese Organization for International Co-operation in Family Planning. He also donated funds to the Draper World Population Fund and was nominated Fund's Honorary Founder. Contributions from JSIF continue to this day. These funds are distributed to promote family planning movements throughout the world.

On 4 April 1977 the Japan Science Society, headed by Sasakawa, co-operated with the Draper World Population Fund to organize the Tokyo International Symposium, "Action Now Toward More Responsible Parenthood." This international symposium was unique, and it drew delegates from many international organizations, national governments, and private population control organizations. The "Tokyo Initiative" that was adopted at this international conference attracted much attention throughout the world. It outlined positive steps to solve unchecked population growth.

Epilogue

ROBERT MULLER
Director and Deputy to the Under-Secretary General for Inter-Agency Affairs
and Coordination, United Nations

To me, Ryoichi Sasakawa is a modern Andrew Carnegie. At the turn of the century Carnegie's brand of philanthropy was visionary, but at that time it dealt with peace mainly in Europe and America, the Western world context.

Sasakawa, on the other hand, sees no national boundaries. He sees the world context. His approach is especially unique because he comes from the rather isolated culture of Japan.

It is my fervent hope that he sets an example, and inspires hundreds and thousands of other citizens of the world.

Sasakawa's historical contribution and his definition of world philanthropy is not only financial but spiritual. He supports world organizations without *restrictions*. I believe that his philosophy of unrestricted donations to be the spiritual aspect of his philanthropy. I am also convinced that this is the most important global perspective on peace.

At this writing I do not believe there exists one other foundation or philanthropist which helps the world as a whole, irrespective of geography, ideology, political or religious considerations. Most existing foundations today have a national base; those few with an international base are limited to a certain number of countries. Mr. Sasakawa's novelty is his support of the world-wide organizations of the United Nations: this makes him a *world* philanthropist.

As I look out of my window today, aware of my own experiences over the last thirty years with the United Nations, I think one of the most important future vehicles for peace will be global thinkers putting ideas into action. If Mr. Sasakawa's actions as a world philanthropist were multiplied, imagine the beautiful results. An uplifting and positive message for everyone around the world would begin to be heard. Wouldn't it be a change from the news we hear today? I firmly believe that *belief* in peace gives it a chance of happening.

Perhaps the time has come for a World Foundation to which people from all nations would be able to contribute without national jurisdictions. New rules would have to be determined. But what if a tax-exempt Foundation with the legal blessing of the United Nations could be structured? This would be one of the most worthwhile projects to be undertaken at this stage.

Ryoichi Sasakawa is devoting his life to peace. And he should march full steam ahead to encourage others to become world philanthropists. To become global thinkers. To understand that mankind is one family.

For this family to enter an era of world peace, we must get into a world of global philanthropy.

Major Positions and Honorary Titles

Chairman, Japan Shipbuilding Industry Foundation
Chairman, Federation of Prefectural Associations of Motorboat Racing
Chairman, Japan Foundation for Shipbuilding Advancement
Chairman, Japan Motorboat Association
Honorary Chairman, Japan Civil Aviation Promotion Foundation
Honorary Chairman, Aircraft Nuisance Prevention Association
Honorary Chairman, Airsafety Association
Chairman, Blue Sea and Green Land Foundation
Honorary Chairman, Japan Education Centre for Hotel Industry
Chairman, Society of the Memorial Services for All War Victims
Chairman, Japan Disabled Veteran's Association
Honorary Chairman, Kasuga Kensho Kai
Chairman, Japanese Foundation for the Promotion of Maritime Science
Honorary Chairman, Japan Science Society
Honorary Chairman, Japan Society for Promotion of Inventions
Chairman, Association for the Space Science Exposition
Chairman, Japanese Fire Protection Association
Chairman, Association for the Promotion of Japanese Traditional Arts
Chairman, Federation of All Japan Karate-do Organizations
Chairman, World Union of Karate-do Organizations
Chairman, World Shorinji Kempo Organization
Honorary Chairman, All Japan Kendo Dojo Federation
Chairman, Japan Racing Pigeon Association
Honorary Chairman, Japan Music Promotive Foundation
Chairman, Life Planning Centre
Chairman, Sasakawa Memorial Health Foundation
Honorary Consul-General of the Kingdom of Tonga in Tokyo
Honorary Consul-General of the Central African Empire in Tokyo
Honorary citizen of Minoo City, Osaka
Honorary citizen of Manilla City, Philippines
Honorary citizen of Managua City, Nicaragua
Honorary citizen of Bandung City, Indonesia

Japan Shipbuilding Industry Foundation

Statement of Support for Fiscal Year 1979
(Fiscal Year—April to March)

	Number of projects supported	Amount
Subjects for Support *Service for Shipbuilding*		
Loans to development of ship-building technology and industry	1,040	Y33,363,600,000 ($166,818,000)
Subsidies for development of technology and dissemination of scientific information and promotion of shipbuilding projects	108	Y5,977,052,000 ($29,885,000)
Services for Marine Disaster Prevention Activities	39	Y1,437,984,000 ($7,189,920)
Dissemination of information concerning maritime affairs	19	Y426,210,000 ($2,131.050)
Promotion of tourism	22	Y339,499,000 ($1,697,500)
Promotion of physical training	34	Y1,025,738,000 ($5,128,700)
Education	42	Y858,721,000 ($4,293,600)
Social welfare	210	Y9,006,290,000 ($45,031,450)
Other public welfare services	148	Y6,275,090,000 ($31,375,450)
Total Funds		Y68,202,529,000 ($340,101,204)

Japan Shipbuilding Industry Foundation

Overseas Support for U.N. etc.
(Category 1 and 2 Grant)

	PROJECT	DONEE
1	Donation for relief of the displaced persons in East Bengal	(depository) United Nations (through Ministry of Foreign Affairs of Japan) Food and Agriculture Organization of the United Nations (FAO)
2	Donation for relief of the peoples of the six drought-stricken countries in West Africa	(depository) United Nations Information Centre in Tokyo Food and Agriculture Organization of the United Nations (FAO)
3	Donation to WHO Voluntary Fund for Smallpox Eradication Programme	(depository) United Nations Information Centre in Tokyo
4	Donation for the relief of displaced persons in Indochina and Cyprus	(depository) Office of the United Nations High Commissioner for Refugees (UNHCR) United Nations Information Centre in Tokyo
5	Donation to WHO Voluntary Fund for Smallpox Eradication Programme and Leprosy Programme	World Health Organization (WHO)
6	Donation to UNICEF	United Nations Children's Fund (UNICEF)
7	Donation to UNFDAC	United Nations Fund for Drug Abuse Control (UNFDAC)
8	Donation to UNRWA	United Nations Relief and Works Agency for Palestine Refugees in the Near East (UNRWA)
9	Donation for World Congress of UNESCO Club UNESCO Prize for Peace Education	United Nations Educational, Scientific and Cultural Organization (UNESCO)

UNITS IN U.S.$

1971	1972	1973	1974	1975	1976	1977	1978	1979	Total
32,467									32,467
		37,735							37,735
			17,857						17,857
			66,666						66,666
						200,000	500,000	500,000	1,200,000
				1,003,000	2,000,000	2,330,000	3,300,000	3,500,000	12,133,000
					330,000	660,000	610,000	610,000	22,100,000
						160,000	200,000	200,000	560,000
						130,000	130,000	130,000	390,000
						140,000		1,030,952	1,170,952

	PROJECT	DONEE
10	Donation for "Information Activities to Promote Understanding for the Concept of the New International Economic Order"	United Nations Department of Public Information (UNDPI)
11	Donation for Asian Regional Seminar on the Outcome of the International Conference on Tanker Safety and Pollution Prevention	Inter-Governmental Maritime Consultative Organization (IMCO)
12	Donation for Seafarers' Training Facilities	Economic and Social Commission for Asia and the Pacific (ESCAP)
	TOTAL	
	Donation to Population Crisis Committee	Draper World Population Fund
Other support		
Other donation for relief of disaster		
	GRAND TOTAL	

1971	1972	1973	1974	1975	1976	1977	1978	1979	Total
							1,000,000	250,000	1,250,000
							175,570		175,570
							26,017	227,670	253,687
32,467		37,735	84,523	1,003,000	2,330,000	3,620,000	5,941,587	6,448,642	19,497,954
			339,443		500,000	650,000	750,000	750,000	2,989,443
4,343	15,755	132,453	56,264	435,455	90,827	1,504,455	1,726,755	2,539,227	6,505,534
838	27,775	15,928	21,826	9,993	78,393	36,456	25,798	67,100	284,107
37,648	43,530	1,861,116	502,056	1,448,448	2,999,220	5,810,911	8,444,140	9,804,969	29,277,038

Chronology

4 May 1899	Ryoichi Sasakawa born, second child and first son of Tsurukichi and Teru Sasakawa in Onohara, Toyokawa Village, Osaka Prefecture, Japan.
June 1912	Ryoichi graduates from primary school, age 13.
1914–1918	Japan fights in World War I on the side of the Allies.
1917	Ryoichi meets pilot Kiyoshi Nishide, and runs away.
1919–1920	Sasakawa serves in Army Air Corps, based at Kagamihara.
1921	Sasakawa recuperates from shoulder injury.
18 January 1922	Tsurukichi Sasakawa dies.
1922	Ryoichi Sasakawa elected to the Village Council of Toyokawa for 4-year term.
1 September 1923	The Great Kanto Earthquake disaster.
1 September 1923	Shizue Miyakawa born.
1924	Sasakawa becomes President of Kokubosha (National Defence Company) and subsidizes publication of *Kokubo*.
1925	Universal manhood suffrage is granted in Japan.
1926	Accession of Emperor Hirohito.
1930	World-wide depression; political unrest in Japan.
1931	Sasakawa forms Kokusui Taishuto (People's Party of the Nation).
1931–1932	The Manchurian Incident; Japan forms puppet state of Manchukuo.
1932	Sasakawa forms National Aviation Union.
1933	Japan announces withdrawal from League of Nations.
7 August 1935	Sasakawa is arrested, imprisoned at Osaka Prison.

1936	Japanese Army officers lay siege to governmental centre of Tokyo.
1937	Outbreak of hostilities between Japan and China.
24 July 1937	Sasakawa is released from Osaka Prison.
1937–1939	Isoroku Yamamoto assigns Sasakawa to visit heads of state in Southeast Asia.
1938	Passage of Japan's National Mobilization Bill.
26 December 1938	Sasakawa is acquitted of "so-called" crimes and resumes business, is involved in trade with China.
1939	Political situation in Europe deteriorates; war impending between Axis nations and democracies.
1 September 1939	Germany invades Poland.
3 September 1939	Britain and France declare war on Germany.
1939–1945	Second World War
December 1939	Sasakawa visits Benito Mussolini in Rome.
10 June 1940	Italy declares war on France and Great Britain.
22 June 1940	France surrenders.
September 1940	Formation of the Rome-Berlin-Tokyo Axis.
1940	The Battle of Britain
17 October 1941	General Hideki Tojo becomes Premier and Minister of War.
1941	Japan occupies Indochina; signs neutrality pact with Russia.
7 December 1941	Japan attacks Pearl Harbour on Hawaii, the Philippines, Guam, Midway Island, Hong Kong and Malaya.
8 December 1941	United States declares war on Japan.
11 December 1941	Germany and Italy declare war on the United States.
1941–1945	War in the Pacific

1942-1945	Sasakawa is member of the Japanese National Diet.
1944	Battle of the Philippines.
1944-1945	United States air raids over Tokyo.
6 August 1945	United States drops atomic bomb on Hiroshima.
8 August 1945	Soviet Union declares war on Japan.
9 August 1945	United States drops atomic bomb on Nagasaki.
10 August 1945	Japanese Government offers to surrender if Emperor Hirohito is allowed to retain his throne.
14 August 1945	Japanese Government accepts terms of surrender. General Douglas MacArthur becomes Supreme Commander of Allied Powers (SCAP).
11 December 1945	Sasakawa imprisoned in Sugamo Prison as Class A War Criminal Suspect.
24 December 1948	Sasakawa released from Sugamo Prison, without indictment or trial.
1949	Sasakawa forms *Shirakiku* (Bereaved Families Association).
28 April 1952	End of military occupation of Japan.
6 April 1954	First motorboat race held at Omura Arena, Nagasaki.
1955	Sasakawa becomes President of Federation of Prefectural Associations of Motorboat Racing.
1956	Japan is admitted to the United Nations.
17 January 1958	Teru Sasakawa dies.
1962	Formation of the Japan Shipbuilding Industry Foundation.
1 August 1962	Sasakawa is made honorary citizen of Minoo City.
1964	The Olymic Games are held in Tokyo.
April 1969	Straits of Malacca Council is formed.

1971	United States agrees to return Okinawa to Japanese rule.
June 1973	Blue Sea and Green Land (B & G) Foundation established.
May 1974	Inauguration of Sasakawa Memorial Health Foundation.
20 July 1974	Museum of Maritime Science is opened to the public.
1975	Draper World Population Fund is established by Mrs. Robin Chandler Duke.
July 1975	World Youth Ocean Assembly convenes at Okinawa Expo.
August 1975	Sasakawa becomes President of Science Society.
4–7 April 1977	Tokyo International Symposium is held in co-operation with Draper World Population Fund and Japan Science Society.
September 1977	Sasakawa receives citation from Secretary-General of WHO, Dr. Halfdan Mahler.
January 1978	Oil Spill Prevention Institution established.
15 July 1978	Space Science Exposition is opened for 6 months.
24 March 1979	Space Science Exposition is re-opened for another 6 months.
April 1979	Sasakawa receives scroll of appreciation from United Nations Secretary-General Kurt Waldheim.
17 April 1979	Sasakawa donates cherry trees to New York City.
24 April 1979	U.S. Navy gives "Emily" to Museum of Maritime Science.
May 1979	Sasakawa receives medal from UNESCO Secretary-General Dr. Ahmadou Mahtar M'bow in Paris.
November 1979	Sasakawa addresses UNESCO Peace Forum in Paris.

8 May 1980	WHO announces the total eradication of smallpox from the globe.
16 May 1980	Sasakawa receives key to the City of Los Angeles.
5 June 1980	World Environment Day.
5 June 1980	Sasakawa attends IFIAS (International Federation of Institutes for Advanced Study) as Honorary Chairman of programme "Scanning of Our Changing Planet".
6 June 1980	Sasakawa donates cherry trees to Stockholm.

Glossary

Banzai	hurrah, cheers
biwa	a lute
bonsai	a dwarf pine tree
bugaku	a court dance and music
bunraku	puppet drama
butsudan	a family (Buddhist) altar
furoshiki	a cloth wrapper, scarf for carrying things
fusuma	a sliding door
futon	bedding
genkan	the vestibule
gin ei	poem chanting
go	(the game of) go
gonta	brat
hakama	pleated skirt
haori	kimono
hibachi	a (charcoal) brazier
kabuki	classic Japanese melodrama
Kokusui Taishuto	People's Party of the Nation
koto	harp-like instrument
kuromaku	wirepuller
menko	Japanese boys game
nisei	second generation American-born Japanese
noh	austere drama using ritual chanting
obaasan	grandmother
ofuro	bath
on	kindnesses, a favour; obligation
Oshyogatsu	New Year's
sake	rice wine
sashimi	slices of raw fish
sekihan	rice boiled together with red beans (happy rice)
senbei	rice cracker
sensei	teacher
shakuhachi	a bamboo clarinet
shoji	paper-covered lattice sliding door

sukiyaki	sukiyaki
Taisei Yokusankai	Imperial Rule Assistance Assoc.
tatami	a mat, straw covered reed mat
tempura	fritter
tofu	bean curd
torii	gate (at entrance to shrines)
yutampo	tin containers with hot water, hot water bottle
zabuton	a cushion (floor)
zaibatsu	a (great) financial clique, financial combine

Sasakawa's Grandfather

Sasakawa's Mother

Sasakawa's Father

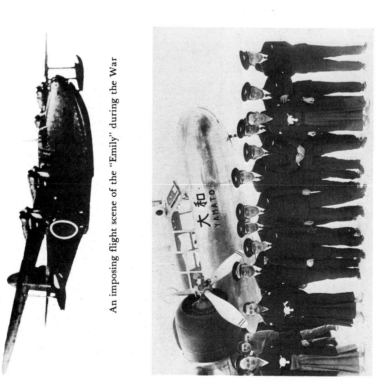

Sasakawa in Air Corps

An imposing flight scene of the "Emily" during the War

Sasakawa with Yamato plane

Sasakawa after Sugamo

Sasakawa before Sugamo

Calling Prime Minister Sato from seabed house

Calligraphy

Motorboat racing

Okinawa Expo, 1975

Space Science Exposition,
1978-79

Sasakawa at General MacArthur's Memorial, Norfolk, 1978

Sasakawa with the King of Sweden

APPENDIX

A REPORT OF
OVERSEAS SUPPORT AND
ASSISTANCE

JAPAN SHIPBUILDING INDUSTRY FOUNDATION
PRESIDENT: RYOICHI SASAKAWA

JAPAN SHIPBUILDING INDUSTRY FOUNDATION
OVERSEAS SUPPORT AND ASSISTANCE (SUMMARY)

DONEE (*DIPOSITORY) PROJECT	FISCAL YEAR	1971	1972
United Nations	Support, Assistance	32,467	
The United States of America	Support, Assistance Disaster Relief Total		
Democratic and Popular Republic of Algeria	Support, Assistance Total		
Argentine Republic	Support, Assistance Total		
Australia	Support, Assistance Total		15,755 15,755
People's Republic of Bangladesh	Disaster Relief Total		
Republic of Bolivia	Support, Assistance Total		
Federative Republic of Brazil	Support, Assistance Disaster Relief Total	4,343 4,343	
Central African Republic	Support, Assistance Total		
People's Republic of China	Support, Assistance Total		
Republic of Colombia	Support, Assistance Disaster Relief Total		
Republic of Ecuador	Support, Assistance Total		
Arab Republic of Egypt	Support, Assistance Total		
Ethiopia	Disaster Relief Total		
Federal Republic of Germany	Disaster Relief Total		4,799 4,799
Republic of Guatemala	Disaster Relief Total		
Republic of Honduras	Disaster Relief Total		
India	Disaster Relief Total		
Republic of Indonesia	Disaster Relief Total		

1973	1974	1975	1976	1977	1978	1979	1980	Total
37,735	84,523	1,003,680	2,330,000	3,620,000	5,941,587	6,448,642	4,842,548	24,341,182
	339,443		500,000	780,000	860,100	1,329,931	1,133,504	4,942,978
			16,600					16,600
	339,443		516,600	780,000	860,100	1,329,931	1,133,504	4,959,578
							17,027	17,027
							17,027	17,027
							500,000	500,000
							500,000	500,000
				12,353			19,784	47,892
				12,353			19,784	47,892
3,752	3,297							7,049
3,752	3,297							7,049
	52,101							52,101
	52,101							52,101
			67,911	1,092,806				1,165,060
1,666					10,206			11,872
1,666			67,911	1,092,806	10,206			1,176,932
					59,203			59,203
					59,203			59,203
							16,939	16,939
							16,939	16,939
							12,616	12,616
						8,324		8,324
						8,324	12,616	20,940
							17,556	17,556
							17,556	17,556
			10,850	10,000				20,850
			10,850	10,000				20,850
3,757								3,757
3,757								3,757
								4,799
								4,799
		3,305						3,305
		3,305						3,305
	16,750							16,750
	16,750							16,750
				20,635		23,036	13,233	56,904
				20,635		23,036	13,233	56,904
			16,852			23,078		39,930
			16,852			23,078		39,930

DONEE (*DIPOSITORY) PROJECT	FISCAL YEAR	1971	1972
Islamic Republic of Iran	Disaster Relief Total		
State of Israel	Support, Assistance Disaster Relief Total		16,361 16,361
Italian Republic	Disaster Relief Total		
Republic of Kenya	Support, Assistance Total		
Republic of Korea	Support,Assistance Disaster Relief Total		
Malaysia	Suport, Assistance Total		
United Mexican States	Disaster Relief Total		
Kingdom of Nepal	Support, Assistance Disaster Relief Total		
Republic of Nicaragua	Disaster Relief Total		3,305 3,305
Kingdom of Norway	Support, Assistance Total		
Sultanate of Oman	Suport, Assistance Total		
Republic of Paraguay	Support,Assistance Total		
Republic of Peru	Support, Assistance Disaster Relief Total		
Republic of the philippines	Support, Assistance Disaster Relief Total		3,310 3,310
Socialist Republic of Romania	Disaster Relief Total		
Republic of Singapore	Support, Assistance Total Suport		
Kimgdom of Sweden	Support, Assistance Total		

1973	1974	1975	1976	1977	1978	1979	1980	Total
				8,279	15,592	8,054		31,925
				8,279	15,592	8,054		31,925
			12,066					12,066
								16,361
			12,066					28,427
			3,340					3,340
			3,340					3,340
							12,351	12,351
							12,351	12,351
34,246		401,337			680,060	57,057		1,172,700
				7,542				7,542
34,246		401,337		7,542	680,060	57,057		1,180,242
						41,067		41,067
						41,067		41,067
3,753								3,753
3,753								3,753
				38,000				38,000
			3,316					3,316
			3,316	38,000				41,316
								3,305
								3,305
							24,038	24,038
							24,038	24,038
52,149	4,163							56,312
52,149	4,163							56,312
7,117		34,118			395,000			436,235
7,117		34,118			395,000			436,235
				41,296	482,392			523,688
	1,779							1,779
	1,779			41,296	482,392			525,467
						159,904		159,904
			17,244					20,554
			17,244			159,904		180,458
			17,683					17,683
			17,683					17,683
				80,000			51,115	131,115
				80,000			51,115	131,115
						200,000	550,000	750,000
						200,000	550,000	750,000

DONEE (*DIPOSITORY) PROJECT	FISCAL YEAR	1971	1972
Taiwan	Support, Assistance Total		
Kingdom of Tonga	Support, Assistance Disaster Relief Total		
Republic of Turkey	Disaster Relief Total	838 838	
United Arab Emirates	Support, Assistance Total		
Socialist Federal Republic of Yugoslavia	Support, Assistance Disaster Relief Total		
GRAND TOTAL		37,648	43,530

1973	1974	1975	1976	1977	1978	1979	1980	Total
				100,000				100,000
				100,000				100,000
9,315								9,315
3,000								3,000
12,315								12,315
		6,688	3,358					10,884
		6,688	3,358					10,884
							16,056	16,056
							16,056	16,056
							13,498	13,498
						4,608		4,608
						4,608	13,498	18,106
156,490	502,056	1,449,128	2,999,220	5,810,911	8,444,140	8,303,701	7,240,265	34,987,089

JAPAN SHIPBUILDING INDUSTRY FOUNDATION OVERSEAS SUPPORT FOR U.N.

DONEE (*DIPOSITORY) PROJECT	FISCAL YEAR	1971	1972
United Nations Secretariat	Relief of the displaced persons in East Bengal	32,467	
	Information Activities to promote understanding for the concept of the New International Economic Order		
	World Journalists' Round-Table Program		
	Total	32,467	
World Health Organization (WHO)	Leprosy Control		
	Smallpox eradication and the expanded program on immunization		
	Special program for research and training in tropical diseases		
	Projects in the Western Pacific region		
	Prevention of Blindness		
	Total		
United Nations Children's Fund (UNICEF)	Services for health and education of children in developing countries		
	UNICEF-assisted projects to supply drinking waters to rural areas in Bangladesh and Indonesia		
	Relief and rehabilitation of water supply component in Lebanon		
	Delivery of drugs to protect young children and pregnant women against malaria in remote areas of Burma		
	Delivery of badly needed school supplies for primary education in Lao People's Democratic Republic		
	Implementation of the national oral malaria project in Bangladesh		
	Total		
United Nations Educational, Scientific and Cultural Organization (UNESCO)	World Congress of UNESCO Club		
	Purchase of one Steinway Concert Piano to be placed at UNESCO Hall		
	UNESCO Prize for peace Education		
	Total		
United Nations Fund for Drug Abused Control(UNFDAC)	Drug abuse control program in developing countries		
	Law enforcement component for drug abuse control in Burma		
	Total		
Office of the United Nations High Commissioner for Refugees (UNHCR)	Relief and rehabilitation of refugees around the world		
	Relief and rehabilitation of Bulmees refugees in Bangladesh		
	Relief and rehabilitation of Afghan refugees in Pakistan		
	Total		
United Nations Relief and Works Agency for Palestine Refugees in the Near East (UNRWA)	Activities to supply food and houses, health care, school education and work training to the Palestine Refugees		
	Total		

96

1973	1974	1975	1976	1977	1978	1979	1980	Total
								32,467
					1,000,000	250,000		1,250,000
							500,000	500,000
					1,000,000	250,000	500,000	1,782,467
		501,800	670,000	900,000	1,100,000	1,100,000	1,100,000	5,371,800
		501,880	500,000	580,000	600,000	500,000	500,000	3,181,880
			500,000	400,000	400,000	400,000	979,616	2,679,616
			330,000	450,000	1,000,000	1,200,000	1,200,000	4,180,000
					200,000	300,000	200,000	700,000
		1,003,680	2,000,000	2,330,000	3,300,000	3,500,000	3,979,616	16,113,296
			330,000					330,000
				330,000				330,000
				330,000				330,000
					360,000	495,000		855,000
					250,000			250,000
						115,000		115,000
			330,000	660,000	610,000	610,000		2,210,000
				140,000				140,000
						30,952		30,952
						1,000,000		1,000,000
				140,000		1,030,952		1,170,952
				160,000				160,000
					200,000	200,000		400,000
				160,000	200,000	200,000		560,000
				200,000				200,000
					500,000	500,000		1,000,000
							200,000	200,000
				200,000	500,000	500,000	200,000	1,400,000
				130,000	130,000	130,000		390,000
				130,000	130,000	130,000		390,000

DONEE (*DIPOSITORY) PROJECT	FISCAL YEAR	1971	1972
Inter-Governmental Maritime Consultative Organization (IMCO)	Asian regional seminar on the outcome of the international conference on tanker safety and pollution prevention		
	Seminar on the survey and certification of ships		
	Total		
Economic and Social Commission For Asia and The Pacific (ESCAP)	Survey of the seafarers' training facilities in Thailand, India and Philippines		
	Aquirement of teaching aids, machinery and equipment for thr seafarers' training institutions in Thailand, India and Philippines		
	Total		
*United Nations Information Center in Tokyo	Relief of the peoples of the six drought-stricken countries in West Africa		
	WHO Smallpox Eradication Programmes in India (WHO Voluntary Fund)		
	Relief of displaced persons in Indo-china and Cyprus		
	Total		
SUB TOTAL		32,467	

1973	1974	1975	1976	1977	1978	1979	1980	Total
					175,570			175,570
							162,932	162,932
					175,570		162,932	338,502
					26,017			26,017
						227,690		227,690
					26,017	227,690		253,707
37,735								37,735
	17,857							17,857
	66,666							66,666
37,735	84,523							122,258
37,735	84,523	1,003,680	2,330,000	3,620,000	5,941,587	6,448,642	4,842,548	24,341,182

JAPAN SHIPBUILDING INDUSTRY FOUNDATION
OVERSEAS SUPPORT

DONEE (*DIPOSITORY) PROJECT	FISCAL YEAR	1971	1972
The United States of America	The Draper Fund of the Population Crisis Committee Assistance of PCC and IPPF activities Seattle Keiro, Issei Concerns (Nursing Home) Contribution for extention of the building University of Michigan ('78, '79), Stevens Institute of Technology ('79) Contribution to help pay travel and living expenses to invite professor from Japan Morehouse College School of Medicine Contribution to support installation of Japanese manufactured electron microscope Nichi Bei Kai Cultural Center (in San Francisco) Contribution for Nichi Bei Kai Cultural Center Building Duke University Fund for operation of a Center for Japanese/Pacific Asian Studies Tulane University Assistance in extablishing and operation of a new medical research laboratory in support of Dr. Arimura's research on Diabetes International Association for Dental Research Assistance of the 58th International Meeting of IADR held in Osaka, Japan San Diego Japanese School Assistance for rent of Trailer Library Linus Pauling Institute of Science and Medicine Assistance in spreading the results of Dr. Pauling's and Dr. Cameron's past research on "Cancer and Vitamin C" Total		
of Algeria	Japanese School Donation of a school bus Total		
Democratic and Popular Republic Argentine Republic	Asociacion Japonesa en la Argentina Assistance in constructing the Nochia Bunka Center Total		
Australia	The Missions to Seamen N.S.W. Donation of buses, a car and other equipment for Flying Angel House Asia and Oceania Thyroid Association Donation in support of the AOTA Workshop Meeting held in Singapore Total		15,755 15,755
Republic of Bolivia	Sociedad Japonesa Assistance in constructing a Japanese Garden Total		
Federative Republic of Brazil	The Memorial Hall in commemoration of the visit of Their Imperial Highnesses the Crown Prince and the Crown Princess of Japan Donation of a 35mm sound projector complete set	4,343	

(Units in U.S. dollars)

1973	1974	1975	1976	1977	1978	1979	1980	Total
	339,443		500,000	650,000	750,000	750,000	750,000	3,739,443
				130,000				130,000
					23,900	58,400		82,300
					86,200			86,200
						150,000		150,000
						250,000	250,000	500,000
						79,856	87,719	167,575
						41,675		41,675
							1,800	1,800
							43,985	43,985
	339,443		500,000	780,000	860,100	1,329,931	1,133,504	4,942,978
							17,027	17,027
							17,027	17,027
							500,000	500,000
							500,000	500,000
						19,784		35,539
				12,353				12,353
				12,353		19,784		47,892
	52,101							52,101
	52,101							52,101
								4,343

101

DONEE (*DIPOSITORY) PROJECT	FISCAL YEAR	1971	1972

Federative Republic of Brazil	The City of Sao Paulo
	  Donation of school equipments
	
	Sociedade Brasileira de Cultura Japonesa
	  Assistance in constructing IMIN SHIRYO KAN
	
	Hospital "Amazonia"
	  Assistance in constructing an annex building
	
	Beneficência Nipo-Brasileira de Sao Paulo
	  Assistance for reconstruction of the center
	
	Total
			4,343

Central African Republic	Government of the Central African Empire Donation of buses Total		
People's Republic of China	Japanese School Donation of a school bus Total		
Republic of Colombia	Japanese School Donation of a school bus Total		
Republic of Ecuador	Japanese School Donation of a school bus Total		

Arab Republic of Egypt	Wafa Wa Amal (Faith & Hope) Rehabilitation Center
	  Donation of 50 wheel chairs
	
	Nandet Abdin Association
	  Donation in support of the association's
	  humanitarian activities
	
	Total		

State of Israel	Israel Disabled Veterans Organization Donation of 50 wheel chairs Total		
Republic of Kenya	Japanese School Donation of a school bus Total		

Republic of Korea	Myung Hwee won (a social welfare association)
	  Assistance in extention of building
	
	Korean Leprosy Association
	  Assistance in construction of the Korean
	  Leprosy Research Institute
	
	Korean Leprosy Institute
	  Donation to support the operation of the
	  Institute
	
	Nazare Won (a social welfare association)
	  Assistance in extention of the building
	  for the aged
	
	Korean Leprosy Association
	  Assistance in producing films for enlightenment
	
	Total		

Malaysia	Tung Shin Hospital
	  Donation of a Ultra High Tension AC Field
	  Medical Therapeutic Device "HEALTHTRON"
	
	Total		

1973	1974	1975	1976	1977	1978	1979	1980	Total
			67,911					67,911
				264,298				264,298
				412,967				412,967
				415,541				415,541
			67,911	1,092,806				1,165,060
					59,203			59,203
					59,203			59,203
						16,939		16,939
						16,939		16,939
						12,616		12,616
						12,616		12,616
						17,556		17,556
						17,556		17,556
			10,850					10,850
				10,000				10,000
			10,850	10,000				20,850
			12,066					12,066
			12,066					12,066
						12,351		12,351
						12,351		12,351
34,246								34,246
		401,337						401,337
					529,801			529,801
					150,259			150,259
						57,057		57,057
34,246		401,337			680,060	57,057		1,172,700
						41,067		41,067
						41,067		41,067

DONEE (*DIPOSITORY) PROJECT	FISCAL YEAR	1971	1972
Kingdom of Nepal	Ministry of Health Assistance for construction of a Leprosy Training Center Total		
Kingdom of Norway	Norsk Sjofartsmuseum Assistance for maintenance and operation of the sailing vessel SVANEN Total		
Sultanate of Oman	Government of Sultanate of Ohman Donation of a dental clinic Car Total		
Republic of Paraguay	Government of the Republic of Paraguay Donation of books "Paraguay y Japon" Leprocomio Santa Isabel Assistance of construction of a Rehabilitation Center Ministry of Public Health Assistance in constructing Centro de Salud Coronel Oviedo (a health center in Coronel Oviedo Total		
Republic of Peru	Fundacion Museo Amano Museo Assistance for operation and maintenance of the museum Sociedad Central Japonesa del Peru Assistance in constructing and operating Centro Cultural Peruano Japones Total		
Republic of Philippines	Hospital of Manila Donation of a new cobalt 60 Teletherapy Unit Total		
Republic of Singapore	National Theatre Assistance to replace and improve the sound system The Singapore Leprosy Relief Association Assistance for extension of annex building for unemplyable ex-patients of leprosy Trafalgar Hospital Donation of two colour TV sets for leprosy patients Total		
Kingdom of Sweden	The International Federation of Institutes for Advanced Study (IFIAS) Donation to support the IFIAS program "Scanning Our Changing Planet" Total		
Taiwan	National Health Administration Donation for the construction of annex building at the Lo-Sheng Leprosarium for rehabilitation, laboratory, class room and conference room Total		

1973	1974	1975	1976	1977	1978	1979	1980	Total
				38,000				38,000
				38,000				38,000
							24,038	24,038
							24,038	24,038
52,149	4,163							56,312
52,149	4,163							56,312
7,117								7,117
		34,118						34,118
					395,000			395,000
7,117		34,118			395,000			436,235
				41,296				41,296
					482,392			482,392
				41,296	482,392			523,688
						159,904		159,904
						159,904		159,904
				80,000				80,000
							50,000	50,000
							1,115	1,115
				80,000			51,115	131,115
						200,000	550,000	750,000
						200,000	550,000	750,000
				100,000				100,000
				100,000				100,000

105

DONEE (*DIPOSITORY) PROJECT		FISCAL YEAR	1971	1972
Kingdom of Tonga	Government of Tonga Donation of an ambulance car Total			
United Arab Emirates	Japanese School Donation of a school bus Total			
Socialist Federal Republic of Yugoslavia	Japanese School Donation of a school bus Total			
SUB TOTAL			4,343	15,755

1973	1974	1975	1976	1977	1978	1979	1980	Total
9,315								9,315
9,315								9,315
							16,056	16,056
							16,056	16,056
							13,498	13,498
							13,498	13,498
102,827	395,707	435,455	590,827	2,154,455	2,476,755	1,787,959	2,384,484	10,348,567

JAPAN SHIPBUILDING INDUSTRY FOUNDATION
OVERSEAS SUPPORT (DISASTER RELIEF)

DONEE (*DIPOSITORY) PROJECT	FISCAL YEAR	1971	1972
The United States of America	Relief of the residents of Teton River area, striken by collapse of Teton River Dam		
	Total		
People's Republic of Bangladesh	Relief of the residents stricken by a large Tornado		
	Prevention of spread of Chorera Disease by a large flood		
	Total		
Federative Republic of Brazil	Relief of the victims in fire of buildings in Sao Paulo		
	Relief of the victims of a local rainstorm in four states in Brazil		
	Total		
Republic of Colombia	Relief of victims of earthquake		
	Total		
Ethiopia	Relief of victims of drought		
	Total		
Federal Republic of Germany	Token of sympathy for the 11 Israelis Olympic team killed in a Palestinian guerrilla attack in Munich		3,144
	Token of sympathy for the victims including German policemen killed by Palestinian guerrilla attack in Munich		1,655
	Total		4,799
Republic of Guatemala	Relief of the vitims of earthquake		
	Total		
Republic of Honduras	Relief of the victims of hurricane		
	Total		
India	Relief of cyclone victims		
	Relief of casualties caused by burst of dam in the town of Morvi in Gujarat State		
	Relief of casualties caused by heavy rain		
	Total		
Republic of Indonesia	Relief of the earthquake victims		
	Relief of the Indonesian island of Lomblen devastated by a tidal wave		
	Total		
Republic of Iran	Relief of victims of earthquakes		
	Total		
State of Israel	Token of sympathy for the victims killed by guerrilla attack by Japanese Red Army		16,361
	Total		16,361
Republic of Italy	Relief of the victims of earthquake		
	Total		
Republic of Korea	Relief of the victims of a local rainstorm in Soeul		
	Total		

1973	1974	1975	1976	1977	1978	1979	1980	Total
			16,600					16,600
			16,600					16,600
3,752								3,752
	3,297							3,297
3,752	3,297							7,049
1,666								1,666
					10,206			10,206
1,666					10,206			11,872
						8,324		8,324
						8,324		8,324
3,757								3,757
3,757								3,757
								3,144
								1,655
								4,799
		3,305						3,305
		3,305						3,305
	16,750							16,750
	16,750							16,750
				20,635				20,635
						23,036		23,036
							13,233	13,233
				20,635		23,036	13,233	56,904
			16,852					16,852
						23,078		23,078
			16,852			23,078		39,930
				8,279	15,592	8,054		31,925
				8,279	15,592	8,054		31,925
								16,361
								16,361
			3,340					3,340
			3,340					3,340
				7,542				7,542
				7,542				7,542

DONEE (*DIPOSITORY) PROJECT	FISCAL YEAR	1971	1972
United Mexican States	Relief of the victims of earthquake Total		
Kingdom of Nepal	Relief of the disaster-striken people of Western Nepal by a Landslide Total		
Republic of Nicaragua	Relief of the victims of earthquake in Maguana Total		3,305 3,305
Republic of Peru	Relief of the victims of landslide occured in Andes Mountains Total		
Republic of the Philippines	Relief of the victims of flood in Luzon Island Relief of the victims of earthquake in Mindanao Island Total		3,310 3,310
Socialist Republic of Romania	Relief of the victims of earthquake in Bucharest Total		
Kingdom of Tonga	Relief of the damage from storm and flood Total		
Republic of Turkey	Relief of the victims of earthquake Total	838 838	
Socialist Federal Republic of Yugoslavia	Relief of the victims of earthquake occurred over the coastal area of Adriatic Sea Total		
SUB TOTAL		838	27,775

110

(Units in U.S. dollars)

1973	1974	1975	1976	1977	1978	1979	1980	Total
3,753								3,753
3,753								3,753
			3,316					3,316
			3,316					3,316
								3,305
								3,305
	1,779							1,779
	1,779							1,779
								3,310
			17,244					17,244
			17,244					20,554
			17,683					17,683
			17,683					17,683
3,000								3,000
3,000								3,000
		6,688	3,358					10,884
		6,688	3,358					10,884
						4,608		4,608
						4,608		4,608
15,928	21,826	9,993	78,393	36,456	25,798	67,100	13,233	297,340